EDUCATION, EDUCATION, EDUCATION

'His humour is a tonic and an inspiration: the sort that has you gnashing your teeth with rage one minute and clutching your sides with laughter the next.'

Rory Bremner

When New Labour came to office in 1997, its commitment to 'Education, Education, Education' captured the imagination of the public. This collection of articles from 1998 to the present day exposes the real state of education during this period, when education policy has never been far from the headlines.

No-one escapes Ted Wragg's sharp-shooting wit: from the 'blamers and shamers' who try to turn teacher-bashing into a national pastime to the 'pale policy wonks' in the Department of Education, who issue regular hare-brained initiatives from the mysterious 'Tony Zoffis'.

Split into seven issue-focused chapters, this hilarious collection will be a tonic for anyone finding themselves unsure whether to laugh or cry about the latest developments in the world of education.

Ted Wragg is Professor of Education at the School of Education, Exeter University and writes regularly in the *Times Educational Supplement*.

EDUCATION, EDUCATION, EDUCATION

The best bits of Ted Wragg

Ted Wragg

RoutledgeFalmer
Taylor & Francis Group

LONDON AND NEW YORK

First published 2004 by RoutledgeFalmer
11 New Fetter Lane, London EC4P 4EE

Simultaneously published in the USA and Canada
by RoutledgeFalmer
29 West 35th Street, New York, NY 10001

RoutledgeFalmer is an imprint of the Taylor & Francis Group

© 2004 Ted Wragg

The views expressed in this book are those of the author and are not necessarily the same as those of *The Times Educational Supplement.*

Typeset by Saxon Graphics Ltd, Derby
Printed and bound in Great Britain by TJ International, Padstow, Cornwall

British Library Cataloguing-in-Publication Data
A catalogue record for this book is available from the British Library

Library of Congress Cataloging in Publication Data

Wragg, E. C. (Edward Conrad)
    Education, education, education : the best bits of Ted Wragg / Ted Wragg.
        p. cm.
    ISBN 0–415–33550–7 (Hardback : alk. paper) -- ISBN 0–415–33551–5
(Paperback : alk. paper)
    1.   Education--Great Britain.   I. Title.
    LA632.W78 2004
    370′ .941--dc22

ISBN 0-415-33550-7 (HB)
ISBN 0-415-33551-5 (PB)

Contents

Introduction

I try to keep a straight face. Goodness knows, I try. But how can you stop yourself doubling up with mirth at some of the capers that go on in education? Even with an iron willpower, it would take a heart of stone not to laugh at the endless stream of wheezes that are launched on a weekly basis. Who would have dared make a joke about the government setting up two committees to look at the problems of duplication, until it happened in real life?

People often ask me where I get the ideas for the satirical columns I write in the *Times Educational Supplement*. I just open the morning post and read the daily newspapers. There it all is: the full-scale Ofsted inspection of the school that only had one part-time pupil (100 per cent of parents thought this, 0 per cent believed that, the report faithfully concluded); the proposal that head teachers should give on-the-spot fines to the parents of truants, presumably sell-otaping a ticket, like traffic wardens do, on to their foreheads, at considerable risk to their front teeth; the requirement that schools in some of the poorest parts of the country should raise £50,000 if they want specialist college status – robbing the poor, like Robin Hood in reverse.

The sixty-three articles in this collection were written during the period when a Labour government completed its first administration and moved through its second, still under Prime Minister Tony Blair's slogan 'Education, education, education'. They came up with a number of good ideas, but then spoiled the effect with some lyrical lunacy. Like the Conservatives before them, they offered a rich seam for satirists. If you set up a large wheeze factory inside the Department for Education and Skills, it is hardly surprising that, alongside some decent proposals, a middling amount of dross will also appear. Pale-faced policy wonks sitting in attics a million miles from the action are not the best people to generate ideas that have credibility. I once upbraided a minister for the rubbish that arrived on head teachers' desks every week. 'That's only what gets out,' he replied, 'You should see the stuff I stop.'

So in this collection I write about heads buried under bureaucracy and barmy, unrooted schemes; mad assessment disease, as 24 million exam papers have to be marked inside three weeks every summer; attempts to turn people into compliant machines, teacher as Dalek; and the voracious government machine, centrally driven by the Prime Minister's own Number 10 policy unit, with everyone else rotating neatly around it, like the solar system. If politicians ever feel the desire to give up direct control of education, I would welcome it with open arms. But if not, then I can only beg that they please keep it coming in all its lunatic richness. Satire is easy nowadays. Just copy out official documents and the world convulses with mirth.

Ted Wragg

one

The wheeze factory

The Great National Wheeze Factory is a complicated web of inter-locking units, rather than a single entity. Until some cartographer draws up a definitive chart of the whole intricate nexus, I have had to construct my own road map.

Wheezes originate from an attic inside the Prime Minister's policy unit and within the Ministry. A large army of policy wonks, pale and drawn-looking after a lifetime working under artificial light, compete with each other to generate artificial schemes which have few roots in professional practice. Ideas are then passed to the refining plant, where the more sensible are stripped

out. The remainder are signed by ministers and sent to schools, where the majority are immediately shredded.

Alongside this cottage industry are the enforcers. Government spin doctors in the Ministry of Truth assiduously weave a web of fiction about how brilliantly successful every initiative is, and if it isn't working, how incompetent everyone else must be. The Office for Standards in Education is the police force, descending mob-handed on schools to make sure there is compliance. The government's idea of a superhead is someone whose job it is to keep a small cluster of half a dozen or so underling heads 'on message'. The whole edifice is a tall thin triangular structure, with each layer controlling the one beneath, desperate to ensure that the wheezes are implemented.

Meanwhile head teachers, anchored in the reality of their daily task, try to resist the pressure to be the final element of the endlessly grinding state sausage machine. Sadly some cave in under the pressures. But the good news is that most have found a way of practising cheerful subversion to keep their colleagues sane and their school on the rails.

Madness dressed as method

Certain new ideas in education make you pause for breath. There was once a proposal that children should lie on the floor while fellow pupils drew round their body outline. The resulting drawing was then supposed to be labelled with the explicit names of body parts. For me and the rest of the beetroot-faced generation of teachers the labels would have read 'thingy', 'whatsit', or 'plumbing'.

Now there is a suggestion that if boys dressed up as girls in infant schools it would help improve their literacy. No it wouldn't. It would probably give them a lifelong identity crisis.

I can remember some of my own aspirations at the age of 5. Donning a dress, hair slide and sensible round-toed sandals with a buckle was definitely not one of them. Learning to read, yes. Catching a stickleback, yes. Scoring a goal past 5-year-old Tony Binns, second in prowess only to the England goalkeeper in our eyes, yes. But cross-dressing did not figure.

In fact, even my dad, who was reluctant to appear in our school but might have rolled up if it had been burning down, would have overcome his bashfulness in front of professional people and gone in to complain about his lad being turned into a Jessie. He would have been joined by a few hundred others.

I know that boys currently lag behind girls in reading, but adopting one superficial feature of a more successful group and trying to transplant it is not the answer. It is like the naive assumption that children in Pacific Rim countries do better in maths because they sit in rows, so we must do the same, which is about as plausible as suggesting that we eat more rice.

The 'take a single feature of a stereotype' explanation of events is completely misconceived. I once heard a university history lecturer propose that some of the more bellicose nations went to war so frequently because they slept on hard beds and never ate a proper breakfast, so they were permanently bad tempered. The thought that shipping them millions of foam rubber mattresses and plates of bacon and egg might have avoided several gory battles was too hilarious to contemplate.

On the other hand, perhaps we should not dismiss this kind of explanation too readily. Have you noticed that virtually all successful and wealthy businessmen wear a tie? If the many talented women working in business and commerce, whose progress has been barred by prejudice, started wearing a sober striped tie, or one with a badge on it, maybe they would do just as well. Maybe not, if the real reason for success in business is having attended a boys' public school.

SCOFF NOT. IT MAY JUST WORK. Nor should we too easily rule out new ideas in education just because they appear dotty at first sight. Really imaginative proposals often seem bizarre, but it is their unusual nature that makes them succeed where others have failed. So I've been thinking up some really eccentric wheezes. Scoff not. They may just work.

Here are my top ten creative and offbeat ideas for obtaining success in the classroom, with a bit of cross-dressing thrown in:

- Always wear skis when you teach Latin.
- Tell your class you are really Alan Shearer if you're a woman (remember to wear a number 9 shirt), or one of the Spice Girls if you're a man (try 'Scary Spice', or 'Terminator Spice').
- Insist that pupils refer to the head as 'Marmaduke', even if she's female.
- Explain difficult concepts with your eyes crossed.
- Make children stand on their heads when teaching them about Australia.
- Never use a green biro for marking work, except in April.
- Dress up as a different *Star Wars* character every day and sign your name as 'Jabba the Hutt' on school reports.
- Quietly hum the *Marseillaise* while correcting spelling errors.
- Take a baby giraffe into your lessons.
- Dress as a member of the opposite sex during school inspections.

Must dash now and get changed. These tights are killing me.

28 May 1999

Re-inspected to destruction

Have you heard of the process known as 'testing to destruction'? It is used on materials and constructions to discover their breaking point. You keep piling on the weights, shearing forces, or whatever, until something disintegrates. Then you know where to strengthen it, or what limits to put on its usage.

I used to think this was purely an industrial process, until I realised that it applied in education as well. Teacher training in universities is currently being inspected to death. There are primary sweeps and secondary sweeps and then, sometimes within months, re-inspections.

Did I say 're-inspections'? Sorry, that should read 'further inspections'. When inspectors come back a year later to do a place over yet again, even if it got top grades, they are not 're-inspecting'. Oh no. Wash your mouth out with soap and water for even using the word. In order to avoid any suggestion that Ofsted might not know its fundamental orifice from its elbow, we are told it is a 'further inspection'.

In my one-man attempt on the British all-comers' records for these things, I was inspected by ten different inspectors in slightly over a year. My son, training to be a teacher, was inspected at the same time by a trainee inspector.

As he carried out his lesson, the teacher watching him was being observed by a trainee inspector, who was in turn being observed by an old-hand inspector. They needed the sort of finishing gantry the judges used to have at the end of sprint races. He said he felt like the smallest bit of plankton at the end of the food chain.

Now, a mere fifteen months later, clearly experiencing withdrawal symptoms, they are coming back again. My son's course is over, so any Ofsted specials, like family discounts or half price for kids, are just too late.

I've tried. Goodness knows, I've tried. I've sent photos and videos of me and the kids to Ofsted, but there are still inspectors in classy detoxification clinics at this very moment, suffering cold turkey because they haven't seen me or my family for days. The cost of these repeated pilgrimages back to the dark caverns in which I and fellow teacher trainers practise our devilish arts must be millions.

During the summer Ofsted was given responsibility for inspecting pre-schools and further education, so the whole of human life is now inspected by the same dreary outfit. This Brian Rix farce, with its incessant opening and closing doors, is only rescued because many of the inspectors are intelligent people who refuse to turn into Daleks and do their best to humanise a mechanical process.

My mother, at the age of 88, is about to go into an old people's home. As she sits there, quietly knitting slippers with big needles, I

THE ULTIMATE OFSTED DREAM

fully expect some cheerful Charlie, with a briefcase marked Ofsted, to roll up and inspect the oldest member of the family to see if she is 'generally sound', at or above the national average.

However, there is one element of the human cycle that seems to have escaped the clutches of Ofsted. So far as I know they have not yet been given the responsibility for inspecting morgues and cemeteries. This seems a regrettable omission in their ever-expanding brief, which I hope will soon be rectified.

Imagine the scene. Ivor Clipboard, Dip. Insp. (El Dorado hotel, Clacton, 1996), arrives at the local slabhouse clutching his 397-page Morgue Inspection Framework. Let the bureaucracy commence.

'How many of the clients are dead?'
'The lot. In terms of mortality, every single stiff is exceedingly deceased.'
'Pulse rates?'
'Uniformly zero.'
'What is the nature of the coffins?'
'All caskets fit exactly.'
'I'll be back again tomorrow to see if they are still dead.'

Inspecting morgues would fulfil the ultimate Ofsted dream. No problems about people being above or below the national average. All would manifest the same degree of deadness. No action plans and special measures would be necessary, because corpses would be incapable of any action.

Everyone would come out at the national average, the ultimate state of uniform conformity. Also, no one would answer back. It's something to look forward to, anyway.

17 September 1999

Retiring under a hail of bullets

'Hello, it's Jenkins here, Swineshire LEA. Is that Swinesville Comprehensive? Can you put me through to the head please?'

'Speaking.'

'Ah Brian, just the man. Did you see that headline in the TES, the one that said "Jaded heads will be paid off"? Only I'm ringing round a few heads in the right age bracket to see if they'd like to take early retirement under this new government scheme. Now I know you're still full of beans, but you did say in your presidential address at the heads' annual meeting that you fancied going early, buying a cabin cruiser and naming it *Lump Sum*.'

'Well I had thought about early retirement, provided there was some enhancement of course, but what's involved?'

'It's fairly straightforward, Brian. You get up to fifty grand in your pension fund, provided that you're a head teacher who, in the government's own words, "is not able to carry forward the major changes envisaged in improving education". Since that includes every single head in Swineshire, County Hall telephone lines have been in meltdown all week.'

'So what exactly would I have to do?'

'We have to be careful here to follow the rules, especially after that fool Simkins at East Swineshire College tried to jump the gun.'

'I didn't hear about that. What did he do?'

'Well you know Simkins, ever the smartypants. He decided to try and beat the rush on a disciplinary rap, so he jumped the visiting inspector and started snogging her in front of all the kids.'

'And he got early retirement on the grounds of stress.'

'No, we gave it him on the grounds of failing eyesight. You see Brian, we've got to be careful how we go about it. For a start, heads can't retire if their school has failed Ofsted, so that rules out most of them in this LEA. For those schools that are eligible we're just going to get Woodhead to sign a piece of paper stating, "This school passed Ofsted but the head is complete shite." Basically you have to prove you're brassed off with reform, which means the door's wide open.'

'You said heads were supposed to be unable to carry forward "major changes" that are coming up. What are these actually?'

'Who knows Brian, who knows? There are so many initiatives

coming into County Hall these days, each containing about a hundred bullet points. We've had more bullets flying round Swineshire schools than were fired at the Battle of the Somme. It could be a compulsory course on pole vaulting at all key stages, or you might have to take assembly wearing a loincloth. Nothing would surprise me nowadays. You've just got to prove you can't cope with them.'

'So how can I prove that?'

'It's easy. Take performance-related pay, for example. I suggest you come up with a completely barmy scheme. Say you'll give a bonus to teachers who can do a headstand in their lessons and whistle the national anthem at the same time, that sort of thing. Or decide that all Chelsea supporters are automatically ruled out, or your name's got to have the letter Z in it. Just think of something that suggests you haven't got the hang of a particular policy.'

'But if I do take early retirement, even with enhancement, I would still be a bit short financially, wouldn't I?'

'No problem, Brian. We've devised a clever scheme that's cracked it. The accounts people have worked out that if you invest your lump sum, and because you'd stop paying superannuation and all those other deductions, you'd only be a few quid short on your bottom-line take-home pay. So we then re-employ you as the lollipop man outside your own school and, bingo, you're back to what you were earning before, but for only a couple of hours a day seeing kids across the road.'

'It sounds marvellous.'

'It is, Brian. But there's one snag.'

'What's that?'

'There's yet another government initiative entitled "Tough new performance criteria for school premises perimeter traffic management personnel". You'll have to get a BA in pedestrian crossing supervision first, before we're allowed to issue you with a lollipop.'

26 November 1999

Big words can mean so little

> 'COMMITTEE'?
> No problem. Two 'm's, two 't's, two 'e's.
> 'MNEMONIC'?
> You won't catch me with that old chestnut. There's an unsounded 'm' at the beginning.
> 'MILLENNIUM'?
> Two 'l's and two 'n's, comes from the Latin 'mille' and 'annus'. Easy peasy. I was spelling it correctly years before they invented it.
> 'PSYCHOLOGY'?
> Come on squire, is that the best you can do? Give me some hard ones.

I love spelling. You know that smug annoying pedant who goes all round the country inserting in biro the missing 'm' in the word 'accommodation' on notice boards? Well it's me, Sid Spellcheck. It's a long unremitting slog, tracking down dozens of signs in guest-house windows, hundreds of neatly mistyped postcards outside newsagents, but it's worth it.

Some people put 'spelling' and 'imaginative writing' in opposition to each other, as if we can only have one but not the other. Anyone who believes that if children learn to spell correctly they will, as a consequence, write mechanical rubbish is an idiot. Of course the two can coexist. It is a question of balance and manner of teaching.

So on the whole I welcomed the publication of an official list of spellings that children should know by a certain age. What worried me was what some people, including teachers, parents and pupils themselves, might do with these words.

When I left school to go to university I was fascinated by American paperbacks with titles like *Words of Power*. 'Language is power,' thundered the blurb on the jacket. 'Increase your word power and you too can go right to the top.' There followed a couple of hundred pages of exercises in vocabulary building, containing words I had never met before, like 'rodomontade'.

'I'll have some of that,' I thought to myself, cheerfully forking out my four and sixpence. There was a problem, however. The words were completely detached from real life or natural usage.

There I was, first person in the family to go to university, eager to impress people, nursing a modest desire to rule the world using my newly acquired 'words of power', but I could never remember what most of these farcically obscure words actually meant, or even whether they were nouns, verbs or adjectives.

I just didn't have the brass neck to drop them casually into essays or conversations. 'Did you see the City game? I thought their keeper was a bit rodomontade. No, not really rodomontade, more gallimaufry.'

Language is dynamic, rooted in context, rich in history, meaning and cultural association; not inert, detached, bloodless, desiccated. I would hate to see schools teaching 'words of power' in isolation. The results would be bad for teachers, children and indeed for the English language.

One of the words on the official list for 11-year-olds is 'agora-phobia'. I can spell it and thought I knew what it meant: two Greek words 'agora' (open space) and 'phobia' (fear) stuck together. Presumably some petrified teacher, spotting an Ofsted inspector, sprinted out of Athens marketplace one day screaming 'Let me out of here' and a new word was born.

It was only when a close relative developed a stark terror of open spaces following the tragic death of her son that I found out what agoraphobia really meant. It was one thing to spell it, but quite another to live it.

Of course we cannot wait until we understand everything fully before learning to spell, but it does help if the words actually have meaning and are learned in a context. I once visited an American school where each class had a 'word of the day', but all they did was spell it publicly every hour or so. Parents had to do the same in the evening.

In one class the current word was 'radiator', in another 'photosyn-thesis'. Imagine the contrived family conversations if you had two children in the school: 'Now Marmaduke and Felicity, don't put that plant behind the radiator, r-a-d-i-a-t-o-r, you'll ruin its photo-synthesis, p-h-o-t-o-s-y-n-t-h-e-s-i-s.'

Pso it could all get very psilly. I hope people are psensible about learning to pspell individual words in isolation. Otherwise I shall just have to give them a damned good rodomontade gallimaufry.

4 February 2000

The wizards of Swineshire

As Harry Potter mania swept the land and people speculated about the contents of the latest book in the series, I realised that these are not pieces of fiction at all, but rather a series of real-life reports on Hogwarts City Technology College in Lower Swineshire.

In case you do not know the stories, here is the background, gleaned partly from the books and partly from the school's Ofsted reports. Like other specialist schools they had to raise a few grand to match the government offer of cash for specialising in wizardry and magic. The head, Professor Albus Dumbledore (Order of Merlin, First Class, BEd in woodwork and PE, Swineshire Academy), was recruited from industry where he had established an enviable reputation for discovering the twelve uses of dragon's blood.

The chairman of governors (Alf Ramsbottom, Ladybird Book 4b) was convinced Dumbledore would help the school move up the league table and that if all else failed he could turn Ofsted inspectors back into human beings. He fervently hoped that the application of dragon's blood would ensure that the school met its target of pupils getting five Wizarding levels A★ to C at GCSE.

NO SELECTION, READ MY ...

Hogwarts CTC has an interesting admissions policy. The best wizard families put it down as their first choice, but it is also allowed to recruit non-wizards (Muggles) if they are of high ability ('No selection, read my . . . aaaaargh!').

The more you inspect the Harry Potter series, the more you realise that Hogwarts CTC is actually an experimental school run by the Standards and Effectiveness Unit of the Department for Education and Employment. For example, it has a house system (bring back traditional values) and fierce inter-house matches of Quidditch, a game played on broomsticks.

This is clearly a government policy to improve our national football team after its disastrous defeats in Euro 2000. Since some of the players could not pass a football accurately to a rhinoceros standing three feet away, and others are as skilful on the ball as an elephant in tights, a bit of magic is called for.

Harry Potter is half wizard and half Muggle (Mudblood). Poor old Dumbledore the head has trouble with pushy parents of old wizarding families who want to keep Mudbloods out. Is this not every school you have ever been in?

Unconvinced? Well what about the 'Dementors', creatures who stare at you, drain away your self-esteem, get inside your head, paralyse you, and the unmentionable adversary simply known as 'he-who-shall-not-be-named'? Does this not remind you of the Office for Spells in Education? If you put a foot wrong your wand is broken in half (i.e. you are put into special measures). No ambiguity there, I would have thought.

Then there are the messages sent by owls. The rude ones, which the owls scream, are called Howlers. Think about the morning mail and official correspondence haranguing heads about staff illness, not meeting targets, neglecting pupils' writing, wasting time after SATs in July, not having counted up how many perforations there are in each toilet roll? Look out of the window and you will see a large bird fluttering down the drive. To-whit to-whoo.

Still doubtful? What about the ghost who teaches the history of magic? Don't you remember him before the introduction of the national curriculum, and before he filled in his threshold application, when he was a fine figure of a man, skipping up the drive with a smile on his face? Now there is such a teacher shortage he has died on the job and been allowed to stay on posthumously.

What about the Mirror of Erised ('desire' spelled backwards), in which you see whatever you want? Be honest, that must remind you of every mission statement and school development plan ever written and every speech to parents ever delivered: 'All pupils developed to their full potential . . . children learn to tolerate and respect one another . . .'

There is one consolation. If you transgress in Hogwarts and your wand is broken, you are still allowed to use the bits. Could be handy for turning someone into a toad if you don't get through the pay threshold.

7 July 2000

Choose bog-standard diversity

Wheeeee! Look out! Here come the spinners. 'Googlies', 'offbreaks', 'legbreaks', 'flippers', to steal the argot of cricket, will come whistling past your ears over the next few weeks as the image-makers' spin and counterspin dominate the mass media. The sillier the process, the more the non-spinners will soar in public esteem.

I was glad that both David Blunkett and John Prescott were quick to disown the notion of the 'bog-standard' comprehensive. It was a demeaning term, usually applied to simple objects. It should never have been used in the first place by Mr Bogstandard, the government's chief spinologist, because it was wrong. The day I see two identical schools is the day I will cartwheel the length of the High Street.

So what is identical and what is different about schools? They follow the same national curriculum, the same tests, and primary

SIMILARITY, YES; IDENTITY, NO

schools are all supposed to have the same structure for their literacy and numeracy hours. These things, you will note, have been externally imposed by successive governments, so are we also to see the end of the bog-standard literacy hour?

Inside these structures the people, textbooks, equipment, teaching strategies are all different. I have never seen two identical lessons: similarity, yes; identity, no. Try teaching theoretically the 'same' lesson to two different classes. Before long someone has asked a question, or given a different answer, and the two supposedly identical lessons are already diverging.

Let us try and construct two identical schools. The head of Regular Comprehensive is Mr Silas Bogg; in charge of maths is Ms Elspeth Standard. Down the road Normal Comprehensive has Ms Elspeth Bogg as head and Mr Silas Standard runs the maths department.

Damn! Different already. Never mind. Let us suppose that both Regular and Normal Comps have 1,200 pupils, assigned to forty classes of exactly thirty pupils each. All the boys are called Nigel and the girls Felicity. Each pupil is of average height and weight. All the teachers like sausage and mash best, play badminton after school and spend their lunch break filling in crossword puzzles.

All pupils were born on 29 January. Everyone has an IQ of 100 precisely, lives 600 metres from the school in a multi-storey block of flats with a blue door (on the top floor, come to think of it), owns a cat called Gerald, and . . . er . . . supports Aston Villa. Not easy, this bogstandardry, is it?

It is actually the differences between schools that make them such interesting places. Diversity is well worth celebrating and extending. I am in favour of giving schools extra cash to develop something of which they are proud, though to suggest that this is the only worthwhile area they cover would be an oblique insult to everyone not engaged in the endowed field of activity.

But an important question needs to be answered first. Are we really in favour of diversity? The Conservatives claimed they were and then made everyone do the same curriculum and tests, even told schools how to fill in the attendance register, their school reports and what colour the deputy head's Hush Puppies should be, though the memory may be playing cruel tricks on this last one.

The present government says it is in favour of diversity, but then imposes the same 15–15–20–10-minute literacy-hour pattern on every primary class. The Japanese and Korean governments, when planning for the new millennium, stated they were in favour of more 'individualism', but would they panic if the aspiration were fulfilled and numerous mavericks began to appear within what have always been ordered societies?

All of this makes one wonder whether 'truth' lies in the rhetoric or the behaviour. If diversity is important, according to spin doctors, then why do the very same artificers become extremely wobbly, turn puce even, when their supporters drift 'off message'?

I think we should embrace diversity wholeheartedly, simply because the alternative is uniformity, a killer concept in education. But if we do so, then we must live with the consequences. A diverse system produces people who can think for themselves.

Good. So diversity it is. That's solved Mr Bogstandard's little problem then.

9 March 2001

On the wrong Gnometrack

I have never been wild about key skills being tackled separately from the context in which they operate. The whole point about these crucial chunks of human competence is that you can apply them in the real world. Intelligent action, sadly, is not really appreciated in our society, unless it is expressed in writing.

For people at work, such matters as literacy, numeracy, social skills are warm blooded and breathing, not dead pieces of parchment in an examination room. The problem with the woeful Teacher Training Agency computerised maths test, offering 15 seconds to do a sum while seated at a computer, is that it bears no resemblance to the context in which decision-making would take place in school. Hire a deputy head to jump up and down on trainees and swear at them if you want reality.

I remember a head teacher a few years ago who was an ace at solving on paper hypothetical problems in an imaginary school. The art teacher has fallen out with the cleaner? No problem. He was all sweetness and light, producing neatly crafted armchair solutions. Unfortunately he was a complete cretin when it came to running his own school: A+ for the armchair theory, D– for the real-world practical.

Now the Treasury has proposed that schools must prepare children to be entrepreneurs. This was followed by demands from enthusiasts that even young children in primary schools should run a business. My heart sank. Surely the wretched Acme Garden Gnome Company was not to be disinterred yet again. I thought it had been safely laid to rest.

For those with a short memory let me fill in the history. There was a craze, a few years ago, for primary children to set up a manu-facturing company. Hours were spent crafting and painting hideous papier mâché gnomes, or other pieces of tasteless junk, which were then sold.

There would have been little wrong with this harmless activity, apart from the disproportionate amount of time some children spent on it, had it not been commercialised. It was the pretence that this was real-world business which spoiled it. Seven-year-old managing directors met earnestly with fellow spotties to discuss whether to invest the meagre profits opening another 'production line' and make even more unwanted artefacts, or just blow the lot on lollipops and call it a day.

Gullible relatives, eager to help children and schools, performed a disservice to entrepreneurship by actually purchasing these debris. It was fun, but it was cushioned, not a genuine business at all: no rent to pay, no electricity bills, no charge for teachers' time. In the cruel world of commerce the Acme Garden Gnome Company would have gone bust. As with pyramid selling and chain letters you soon run out of friends and relatives.

In any case, customers of these futile companies could barely wait until midnight a few days later. In pitch darkness they tiptoed out and dumped their pointless products, as soon as was decent, on the nearest rubbish tip. There the gnomes lay, decomposing in a museum of failed capitalist initiatives, until the next junior entrepreneurial primary school gleefully removed and recycled them.

Real businesses must have a product or service that people feel they need and are willing to pay for over a longer period. I cannot see the point of giving very young people a largely false impression that they have acquired the key skills of the successful trader. Short of inventing a new acne cream, most young entrepreneurs would be better off developing their imagination and industry in school, and applying them later.

The solution, however, is quite simple. The government must now give papier mâché gnomes privileged status. We should immediately set up Gnometrack, a national co-ordinating body for these diverse initiatives.

Then, even if the gnomes explode, melt or cause global warming, huge government subsidies can be poured into the ailing companies. Seven-year-old directors will pay themselves massive bonuses, despite being technically bankrupt, and the European Union can establish a colossal multinational gnome mountain in a cave near Brussels. That's what I would call developing key skills in a real-life context.

29 June 2001

New Year, new paper chase

'That's it, I've had enough.' Santa Claus sounded adamant as he shook the snow off his boots.

'Enough of what, dear?', Mrs Claus replied sympathetically. 'Your toy round? I suppose it must be getting a bit much . . .'

'No, no. That's fine. It's the quality assurance I can't stand.'

'Quality assurance? Of the toys? Or is it something to do with your being chairman of Snowland School governors again?'

Santa groaned as he parked his great boots by the fire, watching the snow on them melt. It was bad enough having had the annual governors' meeting on Christmas Eve, just before his mammoth journey across the world. Now there was to be an additional get-together.

'Some of these people can't have a home to go to,' he protested. 'We've always managed to do the business in one meeting a year. Now we've got to have a special meeting about quality assurance on New Year's Eve, ten o'clock at night. What a stupid idea.'

Santa eased himself back into the soft enveloping luxury of an enormous armchair. He looked out of the window at his giant sledge. Where a few days ago there were thousands of neatly packed presents, it was now stacked high with massive piles of paper. Large snowflakes fell gently on their peaks, forming thick layers of white on white.

'Just look at it. There are forms to fill in about the teachers, the children, the buildings, the library. We'll have to count all the snowflakes landing on the school next.'

'Steady on, dear, you might give them ideas,' replied Mrs Claus philosophically.

Snowland school governors trooped obediently into the resources centre where the head, known as 'Uriah' for his unctuous manner, awaited them with glee. 'I'd like to thank you personally for my performance bonus,' he intoned over and over, shaking individuals vigorously by the hand, drowning each in oil.

Santa could feel the irritation rising. Every year Uriah conned them into upping his salary with some far-fetched yarn about fresh demands, stress, overload, anything. One year he even said he would be leaving, thus securing a huge bonus entirely out of relief. Needless to say his departure never materialised. 'Got to put the school first,' he replied without a hint of irony when asked why he was still around.

Santa cleared his throat. 'Item 1, threshold assessment. Can I ask the head to bring us up to date?'

'I'm delighted to say that we had a 100 per cent success rate. Everyone got their £2,000 bonus.'

'What, even Mr Hardcastle?' Mrs Farnes Barnes shrieked in her high-pitched voice, honed to a fearsome whine after years of childhood elocution lessons. 'You've always said you wouldn't pay him in washers, er, whatever they are.'

'Ah yes, I did try to withhold it, but I'm afraid the external assessor overruled me.'

'Who was the external assessor?' Santa asked. 'It must be difficult to find anyone willing to come all the way to Snowland.'

'It was Mr Hardcastle, actually.'

'Mr Hardcastle?' Mrs Farnes Barnes soared like an eagle up the decibel scale. Santa could feel she was winding up to make one of her legal points. Ever since he had delivered her a Perry Mason video she had fancied herself as an expert.

'Mr Hardcastle? He is not external, so how can he act as adjudicator in his own case? It's *ultra vires*, chairman. I rest my case.'

'No one outside Snowland wanted to do the assessor's job. Mr Hardcastle sent away for the official 125 OHP transparencies and trained himself,' Uriah replied lamely. 'He stood outside my study window when he talked to me and insisted that made him external, claimed it said as much on OHP transparency 112.'

Santa began to feel impatient. There were still several hundred pupil targets to go through.

'Look, we must move on to the pupil part of our quality assurance. Let's make a start on the alphabetical list. What can you tell us about Anthony Abbot?'

Uriah preened himself. 'In return for his threshold bonus, Mr Hardcastle has calculated all our targets, chairman. Anthony Abbot has been set a target of eleven A* grades at GCSE next summer'.

'But he's only 6 years old.'

'Is he? I mean, yes, er, we're trying out this new value-added approach and I think Mr Hardcastle may not have quite got the hang of it yet . . .'

Santa looked on in despair. Quality assurance. He mouthed the two words to himself. Both sounded hollow. Outside the window two of his reindeer, Dancer and Prancer, waited patiently alongside two inspectors, Wally and Clueless, who would eventually deliver all the completed forms to the Ministry of Paper. It was going to be a long night.

28 December 2001

Tips for superheads and menials

Question: How will you recognise superheads who are running several schools?
Answer: You won't, because you'll never see them.

The current notion of having one distant wizard in charge of a cluster of schools sounds terrific. You take five schools currently run by clueless bozos, employ some distinguished genius in red pants, blue tights, big letter 'S' on chest, at a trillion pounds a year, and hey presto, results improve overnight, all five soar up the league table, parents ecstatic, every school in the land performs well above the national average, brilliant.

Unfortunately the reality would be different. The best heads run schools well because they can combine power, responsibility, unique commitment and insider knowledge. Superheads, even if they manage in a collegial style, will disempower the local head. They must be given ultimate power and authority, or why create them? Theirs is a shared, not a sole commitment to any individual school, so their first-hand insider knowledge will be limited.

The theory sounds fine: give lots of schools the benefit of one highly competent person's expertise, protect local head teachers from all the boring bureaucracy and fisticuffs so they can concentrate on running their school more effectively, capitalise on the benefits of size. It sounds like a neighbourhood scheme, each cluster being a tiny local education authority with its own chief education officer.

It is equally possible, however, that creating thousands of weeny LEAs is an inefficient way of running schools. Bureaucracy might increase, as more people have to be copied in about management decisions, time is wasted referring key decisions upwards and waiting for a reply, rather than making them quickly. Teachers will become Mrs Thingy and Mr Whatsit to people responsible for armies of them, while pupils will be A397 and C421.

Still, this looks to be the future, so here is my guide to superheads and their menials: how to run a cluster of schools, or work in one of the satellites, in ten easy lessons.

Tips for superheads

1. To appear to be on top of things, find one tiny detail and query it: e.g. 'I notice that the daffodils in the entrance hall have died', guaranteed to frighten the crap out of the locals, who will think you have a complete grasp of the totality.
2. Say 'yes' frequently when individuals explain something to you, preferably in the middle of their sentences, suggesting you have a quick mind and are ahead of them; in reality, you are musing on whether your new carpet should be red or blue.
3. Choose one member of the support staff at random and say, 'This school would be completely lost without you.' (Supplementary tips: (a) don't say the school would be lost without 'people like you', too lofty and patronising, (b) make sure you are not talking to the head.)
4. Use the royal-family trick of asking standard questions, like 'How long have you been here?' Be prepared for the reply 'Didn't you see the sign saying that all visitors must report to reception and wear a sticker?'
5. Don't try the old technique of telling people, 'I want to know what *you* think we should do,' because they immediately say to themselves, 'Is this what we're paying you a hundred grand a year for?'

Tips for menials

1. Learn to interpret the true meaning of superhead-speak, e.g. 'I'm sorry, I'm terrible on names at the moment, my head is so full of all this administrative rubbish', really means, 'I have absolutely no idea whether you are the window cleaner or the head of astrophysics.'
2. Try calling any bluff, so if the supremo picks up one tiny detail in a long and complex paper, just to impress, respond with, 'I'd be interested in your thoughts on the section on page 5 about teaching strategies . . .' Have a camera ready to capture the facial expression when desperately reading something for the first time.
3. If the superhead ever becomes completely overbearing, practise 'malicious compliance', i.e. fulfil what is required, but to the

limit: 'You did ask for some policy papers, so I just sent the van round because . . .'

4. Say suddenly, as a little joke, 'I think you're in the wrong school; this is Lower Piddlington; Upper Swineshire is the one on High Street . . .' – worth it just for the resulting look of blind panic.

5. If all else fails, staff should wear oldest clothes, put shaving foam on face, look wild eyed, and blubber 'I can't stand it any longer'. This will ensure that the superhead only visits other schools in future.

8 February 2002

two

Cogs in the machine

The final links in the very long chain of command in education are teachers, most of whom feel themselves to be light years away from the Prime Minister's policy unit at the top of the triangle. The result of the wheeze factory's command and control structure is that the people who eventually have to do the job of teaching children on a daily basis must be 'managed'.

Increasingly the preferred style of management has been to treat teachers as machines. Judged to be incapable of independent thought, they must be programmed to obey instructions, tick little boxes, fill in forms. Normally good management would involve maximising the time and energy workers can devote to their task

and keeping their morale high. Treating teachers as Daleks, programmable robots, achieves the exact opposite: time and energy are sucked away, while morale plummets.

In this surreal, mechanised world, teachers and their machines become inseparable. Procedures are computerised, often becoming completely inoperable, as error messages flood the screen: 'You have 15 seconds to complete this form before you are terminated. Bleep bleep.' In desperation, some send for expensive consultants to sort them out, confidence in their own powers of judgment comprehensively shattered. Others soldier on, shrugging their shoulders philosophically from time to time.

Every so often the top of the chain twitches into action and a desperate minister sends out letters to the heads and chairs of governing bodies in 24,000 primary and secondary schools, haranguing them to meet their targets. Racks and thumbscrews are not mentioned by name, but the message is clear enough: the machines must produce more, or the factory will be closed down. It is a rotten way of managing 400,000 professionals, to treat them as if they had no brain. Fortunately the machines have an unprogrammed sense of humour, so most can see the comical paradox: the machines are human; their masters are the robots.

Chains? Pull the other one

After the rich haul in my morning post, I shall never use the expression 'junk mail' again. Just when all seemed lost, at the very moment of darkest despair, I received one of those inspired mail drops, telling about a new journal, which solved all my problems. My life will change, I can feel it.

An attractive little leaflet landed on my desk. It was aimed at various people including 'practitioners working in . . . the provision of public services who are involved in supply chain management'. That's me. We in primary, secondary and tertiary education supply teachers, pupils, you name it, and we are in a chain, so it must be relevant.

'Whatever your area of interest, don't be the weak link in your supply chain,' the leaflet exhorts boldly on its front page. 'Subscribe to *Supply Chain Management: an International Journal.*' I will, I will. You hit a nerve there, *Supply Chain Management*. I don't want to be the weak link in anybody's chain. Rush me a copy immediately.

There is more inside. '*Supply Chain Management* is broad based . . . It covers the key issues including: Electronic Data Interchange (EDI) . . . Efficient Consumer Response (ECR) . . . Logistics Information Technology . . . Purchasing and Supply. You already know the buzz-words.'

No I don't, *Supply Chain Management*. These buzzwords are new to me. I know all the educational bullshit, I mean buzzwords, but I am hungry for new experiences and acronyms that will solve my problems. We in education are eager for a novel science, with accompanying gurus and newspeak, so flood me in soothing clichés, drown me in the kind of jargon that will impress my friends.

Is there a suitable guru, so I can hang on his every word? Please reassure me that there is someone who is acknowledged to be the world's leading expert, the Albert Einstein of supply chain management. Is he a charismatic figure called Norbert Periwinkle of East Pasadena State College, and does he write authoritative but mystical articles entitled 'ECR (Efficient Consumer Response) in the 21st century', or, for novices like me, more rudimentary pieces like 'Logistics Information Technology for Dummies'?

I like to think, *Supply Chain Management*, that, in our amateurish way, we in education may already have some useful experience on which to build. Take the concept of Efficient Consumer Response (ECR), for example. I don't know what the industry standard is in this field, but when teachers used to supervise school dinners, our school record was six minutes from spuds to puds. Hard peas, watery mash, indigestible mince, prunes, lumpy custard, the lot, all consumed in 360 seconds flat, not a Rennie in sight, nor needed. We didn't call it ECR in those days, by the way. It was GTBTF (Get The Buggers Through Fast).

As a raw recruit to this new science, I may have got the wrong idea about supply chain management, but I see one of your articles is entitled 'Beyond MRP – the operation of a modern scheduling system'. First of all let me congratulate the author on being 'beyond' MRP, whatever that is. (More Ruddy Paper? Make Robots Perfect?) It is always a good idea to be 'post' any current fad: postmodern, post-structuralist, postman Pat.

Secondly, we in education have some experience of 'a modern scheduling system'. I came across a head who has two timetables: one for normal use, one for when inspectors are present. The secretary sits on the roof with a telescope and, if a vanload of inspectors is spotted, the mechanical version of the literacy hour is wheeled out. Otherwise the school's common-sense timetable operates. Pretty modern scheduling, you have to admit, and well beyond MRP, I suspect, even though I still do not know what MRP stands for. (My Rump's Purple?)

But I see, *Supply Chain Management*, that your leaflet describes the journal as providing 'the key information resources for everyone involved in the mechanisms of making, moving, buying and selling'. 'Mechanisms', that's it in one.

We've already got performance criteria, curriculum delivery, value added, underpinning knowledge, range statements, flangieform springleboobs, the lot. If you are to take root in public services like education, you may have to get out the weedkiller first.

2 April 1999

Meet the merchants of morale

Fancy earning up to £10,000 a day? If so, you might like to know that there is a new breed of management consultant known as the 'corporate motivator'. Such people are hired by big companies to regenerate tired employees by giving them a bit of zip. Apparently the going rate for a corporate motivator is about £2,000 a day, and some charge five times as much.

These 'new masters of motivation', according to an article in the *Guardian*, leap up in front of the workforce and, er, motivate them. They do this by using similes and metaphors – geese flying in formation, or someone scoring the winning goal. If teachers are as demoralised as is commonly said, then perhaps a few flying geese might help.

One guru says, 'We don't make speeches . . . We increase the vitality of people's relationship with work by engaging them in a lively conversation.' That was precisely what my Uncle Ralph used to do at work, but the foreman just told him off for making jokes about the management and distracting people. Uncle Ralph never earned more than twenty quid a week.

Another wizard tells people to run round the room and smile, as both acts trigger endorphins. Hello funny farm.

According to reports you need a bag of tricks to succeed as a corporate motivator. Trick of the trade number one is to use a clever metaphor, preferably a sporting one. Talk about 'winning the race', 'climbing the mountain', or some such.

Trick of the trade number two is to have a collection of trenchant sayings. One corporate motivator (£2,000 to £5,000 per day) tells his eager audience: 'Opportunity is like a snowflake. When it touches your hand, it's gone.'

I must admit this shrewd observation did fill a significant gap in my scientific knowledge. But he's dead right, you know. Temperature of snowflake – zero degrees Celsius. Temperature of hand – about 37 degrees Celsius. Result of warm hand touching ice cold crystals – snowflake melts. Brilliant. But, short of sticking your hand in the freezer, how do you seize these fleeting chances?

I have decided to set up a new agency for education that will revitalise the teaching profession: Specialist Corporate Academic

Motivators. We at SCAM have recruited the world's finest exponents of talking complete cobblers to the easily impressed for very high fees. Their credentials are impressive, as our glossy brochure reveals.

Fiona Fforbes–Flannel
Specialism: Motivating those teachers who are clapped out, but snobby.
Cost: £2,000 per day.
Subtle similes: 'Children are like champagne: shake them up and they go "pop!"; leave them alone and they go flat.'
Words of wisdom: 'In my experience Tuesday always follows Monday, even when it's wet playtime, but it precedes Wednesday. Friday invariably comes at the end of the school week, and not too soon at that.'

Brian Banality
Specialism: PE teachers who have lost their drive.
Cost: £2,000 per day.
Subtle similes: 'Teaching is like a canoe race: row with the current and you win Olympic gold, row against it and you're up shit creek.'
Words of wisdom: 'If you look back, you'll only see where you've been, but if you look forward, you'll see where you are going. This is particularly important when approaching a cliff edge with a thousand foot drop, or a revolving door.'

Sally Sycophant
Specialism: Crawling to the powerful.
Cost: £3,000 per day.
Subtle similes: 'Getting promoted is like entering a dog show: Rottweilers command respect, **but** poodles are more likely to win prizes.'
Words of wisdom: 'Always obey your excellent head teacher and you will never go far wrong; so can I have the money now please, in used notes, and would you like to book me for another week at ten per cent discount?'.

Samuel Snakeoil

Specialism: Post–inspection trauma.

Cost: £10,000 per day.

Subtle similes: 'A bad school inspection is like a hot air balloon with a slow puncture: one little prick can ruin months of hard work.'

Words of wisdom: 'After your inspection create your own endorphins. Run round the room and smile at the same time. You won't feel any better, but two nice men in white coats will come and take you away for a long rest.'

11 June 1999

Press 1 if you've had enough

The bizarre association of two recurring dislikes flashed across my life
the other day. The first hate is recorded messages, the second is
helplines. I have to use them, but I loathe those indifferent mechanical
voices.

There is nothing more infuriating than ringing a helpline and
getting a recorded message. You are at your wit's end, but all you get
is the speaking clock: 'Welcome to the Acme Infotech helpline. If
your computer is on fire, press 1; if you are so frustrated you are
about to smash it to pulp with a sledgehammer, press 2; for all other
enquiries, press 3.' Sod off.

A research funding body I was applying to has just gone over to
electronic application forms. This would be fine if they had been
conceived with human beings in mind. Unfortunately they are
aimed at deranged Martians with nothing better to do with their
lives than work out how the damned things function.

> 'Hello. Oh thank goodness I've got through at last. Only your
> phone has been engaged for ages.'
> 'Welcome to the research application helpline. I'm sorry I'm not
> able to speak to you at the moment, but if you leave your name
> and telephone number, someone will call you as soon as
> possible.'
> 'You bastard. You unmitigated heartless bastard. I've dialled my
> fingers to the bone to get through and you swan off somewhere
> . . .'

Eventually I got through to a very helpful human being. The reason
we need helplines is because systems have been set up to suit their
begetters rather than their users. Even though I am well used to the
funny ways of computers, my newly acquired friend had to steer me
through a completely meaningless process.

> 'Go into "Settings" and choose "Printers".'
> 'Right, I've done that.'
> 'Now select "Apple LaserWriter II NTX".'
> 'But I haven't got an Apple printer, or an Apple computer, for that
> matter.'
> 'I know. But we're going to fool your computer into thinking that
> you have.'

Oh good. So I'm now reduced to playing practical jokes on my wretched computer.

Even worse are the helpline people who have been on telephone courses, but are otherwise clueless. You can recognise them immediately because they start off with the totally

HOW CAN I HELP? unreal: 'Hello, my name's Damian. How can I help you?' Probably by having a head transplant, is the answer, as Damian is some spotty airhead with a set of written instructions which he will read out in an uncomprehending way. Ask for a 'supervisor' and you get Sharon, who has been there two weeks longer.

So when the new helpline for stressed teachers was announced I did have a few wobbly moments. It is a good idea, long overdue, but how will it work? Will it be like Alcoholics Anonymous, staffed by fellow sufferers who understand?

'Hello, Mephistopheles here. How can I help?'
'Is that the teachers' helpline? Only I'm feeling really stressed and I don't know where to turn. We've got SATs starting tomorrow and . . .'
'Don't tell me. We're the same. Half our staff are in intensive care . . .'

I once thought of founding Teachers Anonymous for people scared to admit that they teach for a living. 'My name's Sally and I'm a teacher.' Thunderous applause and cries of 'Right on!' from fellow sufferers. After series like *The History Man* and *Porterhouse Blue* were shown on television, many of us working in universities went into denial and tried to pretend we were bus conductors.

Will the teachers' helpline be tough in its response, merciless with wimps?

'I'm a head teacher and I'm suffering from acute stress, as our parents are so demanding.'
'Pull yourself together, you snivelling worm. Don't expect any sympathy from me, you pathetic little creep.'
'Er, I think I'm feeling a bit better now, thank you.'

Worst of all, will the new helpline be fully automated, complete with Dalek?

'Hello. I'm absolutely desperate. I'm a stressed teacher and I'm thinking of killing myself.'

'Welcome to the stressed teachers' helpline. If you are planning to shoot yourself, press 1. If you prefer throwing yourself out of the window, press 2. For all other types of suicide, press 3.'

1 October 1999

Tell Sid: beware of flobbabytes

There is a bloke called Sid Cyberspace who is ruining my life. I suspect he is also giving a hard time to everyone else working in education.

Sid is an obsessive twenty-four-hour-a-day workaholic who never sleeps. I don't know what he looks like, where he lives, or what he eats for breakfast. I only know what he does, or rather what he probably does, since I have never met him.

'Did you get my e-mail?'
'What e-mail?'
'Don't say the e-mail is down again. We've been having problems all day.'

That is just one typical example of Sid Cyberspace at work. He spends much of his time tampering with the Internet and e-mails.

Before anyone is awake he is busy typing neat little screen notes with yellow exclamation marks, saying 'connection to server has been severed', 'host not known', and 'all proxies are down'. They are as informative as an Albanian thesaurus to most of us, farcical even, but that is Sid's style.

He used to work for the railways, writing those smeared felt-tip messages on whiteboards: 'Trains to Little Piddlington will be delayed because of operating difficulties in the Greater Piddlington area.' 'Operating difficulties' meant that some poor passenger, driven to desperation by Sid's little japes, had hurled himself off a bridge.

The moment you log on to your computer, Sid Cyberspace will slip in one of his bits of gibberish. As a result you can never be certain that your e-mails have been received, so you send them again, just to make sure. That is why e-mails, like buses, often arrive in pairs.

In offices, schools, universities, I see person after person sitting in front of a screen, staring vacantly. What did people working in education do before computers started to dominate their lives, for goodness' sake? Talk to someone? Read books? Teach?

Why, in former simpler times, did we waste our time on these trivial pastimes? We could have been gazing longingly at our monitor, waiting for Sid's wretched hourglass to go away.

Just when you've had enough and want to close your computer down, escape at long last from the cyberworld and re-enter the real one, blinking uncertainly in the light, rubbing your eyes, wondering who these people with legs and a head are, what does Sid do? He flashes up his bloody hourglass.

So you sit there, open mouthed, hopelessly hooked to the end of time, in my case screaming, 'Come on, shut down, you evil bastard.' When, in sheer desperation, you simply pull the plug, just to get rid of the irritating little icon, Sid waits until the next time you switch on to get his revenge.

'Your computer was shut down prematurely.' Yes, Sid, I know it was. I pulped it with a sledge hammer, so I could get some sleep. It is no good protesting. He will make you run Scandisc, or Rumpelstiltskin or something, before you can play again.

Then you bump into one of Sid's human-form pals, not realising they are his agents. Their job is to tell you that you need an even bigger, faster hard disc and yet more RAM. You've probably got 64 trillion megabytes of junk already, but Sid's mates will talk you into buying another truck load.

The correct scientific term for this phenomenon is 'Sid's Law of Halves'. According to Sid's Law you always have exactly half of what you actually need. You've got 32 flobbabytes? What a pity, Sid's chums will gleefully pronounce. You should have at least 64. Only for a while that is, because once you've got 64, you will need 128.

Unfortunately you cannot outrun him. He is insatiable. He gulps down bowls full of ROM and RAM like cornflakes. In the end you actually phone people to check if your e-mail has arrived. The tinkling noise from your computer is Sid laughing hysterically at the irony of it.

I now know what we in education must do. Each of us should buy a million flobbabytes of everything and ram it all into our computer in a tangled heap. That will show him. If Sid Cyberspace is in there, I hope the spiteful little bugger suffocates.

17 March 2000

Conversations with a machine idiot

I like computers, unless they refuse to work and start displaying 'error' messages, at which point I could cheerfully smash them to a fine mulch with a sledgehammer. Otherwise they are my substitute for never having had a toy train as a child. Beep beep, toot toot. Lovely.

Like toy trains, however, there is a limit to what they can do. The problems arise when they are made to work beyond these boundaries. I have a horror of going into a computerised health-diagnosis program one day and finding I am pregnant. Help, let me out! Where is the nearest real doctor?

The availability of certain online services is a twenty-first-century boon. Everything is available at the touch of a keyboard and mouse. You want a pupil attainment analysis? It's online. Need some factual information about the subject you're teaching? Get them electronically. Fancy a tuna and cucumber sandwich? Press 'Y' and one will no doubt appear round the back of your computer.

You can even take tests online. Unfortunately, as thousands of teacher trainees have discovered trying to do their Teacher Training Agency sums test on the computer, the systems are not yet foolproof.

'If two teachers dig one hole in three hours, how long would it take for one teacher to mark six books? You have 15 seconds.'
'Er . . . I'll have a double burger and large fries please.'
'With or without mayonnaise?'
'Is the answer 30 minutes?'
'Incorrect. Small fries, no ketchup. Level 1.89. Resit required, resit required . . .'

It worries me when printouts and computer diagnoses are given far more credibility than they sometimes deserve. Then the medium becomes the message. Precise-looking figures to two decimal places and a neatly boxed set of results make the whole thing look as if the secrets of the universe are being revealed. Yet if random numbers were fed in the outcome would look just as impressive. It's a machine, damn it.

Modern computer programs are said to be so sophisticated that you are not supposed to be able to recognise you are interacting with a machine rather than a human being. Yes you can. Anyone with any sense knows how these things work.

> 'I'm feeling depressed.'
> 'Why are you feeling depressed, Malcolm?'
> 'The deputy head keeps telling me I'm no good as a teacher.'
> 'Tell me more about the deputy head, Malcolm.'

That is robot speak, as the computer gropes for sense, blindly obeying its machine-coded instructions . . . 'Tell me more about X', feeding back its victim's own phrases. It is very tempting to foul up the whole neat little charade.

> 'I'm feeling splinged.'
> 'Why are you feeling splinged, Malcolm?'
> 'The Obergauleiter keeps telling me I'm no good as a mortuary attendant.'
> 'Tell me more about the Obergauleiter, Malcolm.'

So I feel increasingly concerned about some of the mechanised online services being touted in education. Pupil tests, for example, are almost certain to be yes/no or multiple-choice items, because more qualitative assessments are problematic for programmers. It offers a very limited view of assessment.

Nor am I too convinced about individual pupil predictions and targeting. Some pupils nowadays are being predicted for a hatful of A★ grades at GCSE simply because they did well in their Key Stage 3 assessments. The poor beggars can easily see themselves as failures if they fall short.

Then there are the online teacher-skill diagnostic programs, purporting to assess and improve professional competence, usually on the basis of pupil questionnaires. They have a limited place, but cannot begin to match advice from a skilled observer.

In the end the computer, instead of being the servant, becomes the master, moving education into programmed multiple-choice mode. Knowledge and skills are segmented, dismembered, chopped into byte-sized chunks, served up with ketchup and a large bill.

> 'I would throw most of these online programs in the bin.'
> 'Why would you throw them in the bin, Malcolm?'

**I DON'T
DO IRONY**

'They look more precise than they are and see people as robots. Machines are idiots.'

'Why are machines idiots, Malcolm?'

'A double tripeburger please, with sauce.'

'I don't do irony, Malcolm. That will be £399 plus VAT.'

15 June 2001

Let poison begin with a pee

I love calculators. Never having had a toy train as a child I have always been a sucker for anything with buttons or flashing lights. Playing with numbers is fascinating. We number junkies love doing huge sums in our head and then carrying out massive calculations on a machine in microseconds.

In the early 1970s the set of data I collected for my PhD was so enormous it had to be sent away to the London University Atlas computer for processing, because my own university's mainframe was unable to cope. Today my laptop would handle it without a murmur.

At that time our department wanted to buy a desktop calculator, about the size of an old-style typewriter, for £1,200. A lecturer in the Engineering department advised us to wait. He showed me the first hand-held calculator I had ever seen, a small half brick, purchased in America for a mere £400 and it had four memories. Four memories – wow! Today's equivalent would probably come free with a packet of crisps and weigh an ounce.

It was disappointing, therefore, to read that primary teachers have been criticised by the Office for Standards in Education, among others, for not feeling confident teaching about calculators. I do not blame Ofsted, since its pronouncements are unspun nowadays, but this conclusion was predictable.

In July 1998 calculators were given 'poison' status by Stephen Byers, then Minister for Schools, making a feeble attempt to appear a macho guy taking tough tough tough action (while appealing to traditionalists who might normally vote for another party). Stevel Knievel leapt over twenty metaphorical buses, crying 'Batten down the hatches, me hearties; I tell 'ee there'll be none o' them new-fangled instruments o' the devil aboard this lugger', which was not very clever for someone who thought eight sevens made fifty-four.

Stevel's spin to the press gave the public the impression that the government was actually banning calculators in primary schools. 'Calculator ban marks return to tradition' was one headline. It did nothing of the sort. Advice was simply issued that calculators should be used sparingly in infant schools (surveys showed that this was the case anyway) and that junior-school pupils should understand the processes they were using. These late-twentieth-century tools are commonplace, so it would be folly not to prepare children to use them intelligently and without error.

Nonetheless the damage was done. Primary teachers became apprehensive about offending the mighty. Would calculators have to be used in a lead-lined cellar, while wearing a face mask, and then only when Shrove Tuesday fell on a Friday? Perhaps the sole permitted calculation in class would be to multiply a huge sum by another colossal number so that the letter E appeared in the window, showing that Satan's evil little implement had had a nervous breakdown.

All these political machinations lead me to one conclusion. One way or another teachers will get the blame. Castigate them in 1998 for using calculators in the classroom, then hammer them four years later for not using them.

The Conservatives sold national testing to parents as a means of smoking out poor teachers, saying their over-generous marking would be exposed by objective tests. In the event schools' assessments turned out to be stiffer than the test scores, so the same government simply announced to parents that teachers were failing to recognise their children's talents. It's a dirty world.

So what will be the next somersault? Will a 2003 Ofsted report complain that each numeracy hour, like Caesar's Gaul, is divided into three parts? Will the teaching of literacy be damned as too predictable, because every lesson starts with 15 minutes of shared text? Er . . . surely that is what teachers were told to do, under threat of having their vitals severed and their pensions reduced to three carrots a month.

Funnily enough I doubt it, and the reason is simple. Ofsted inspectors have actually been forbidden from criticising the structure of these hours. There, the truth is out. Shocked? Didn't realise? Can't believe anyone would be so manipulative?

The evidence lies on page 9 of the Ofsted Update of Winter 1997, which commanded inspectors unambiguously: 'While it is right and proper for inspectors to criticise poor teaching and badly structured lessons wherever they occur, schools must not be criticised for adopting the principles and practice required by the National Literacy and Numeracy Projects.'

Just like the Kafka character accused of committing an unspecified offence and then executed, while never discovering what his crime was, you are guilty anyway. Guilty if you smile, guilty if you don't. So what are you waiting for? Take all the school's calculators outside, pile them up in a field somewhere, and then widdle on them, you anarchist.

3 May 2002

Any more bright ideas, then?

I was intrigued at the news that the DfES is setting up an Innovation Unit and appointing a Director of it. After the avalanche of novelties engulfing schools in recent years, what on earth would be the key interview question?

'Do you now have, or have you ever had an initiative?'
'No.'
'Splendid, you're in.'

It will be a challenging assignment. Life is a mixture of the new and the familiar. Novelty is exciting, familiarity is reassuring, so most of us enjoy a mixture. Push the balance too far in one direction and people get upset. Endless innovation can be disorientating, but if life stays the same we become bored and complacent, nothing improves.

The very word 'initiative' is rooted in the Latin for 'beginning', it is only the start. You have to keep running with the best ideas in education over a sustained period, so they take root. When Michael Barber was appointed Dean of New Initiatives at the London Institute, I remember wondering whether there would need to be further appointments, such as Dean of Picking Up Yesterday's Initiative and Kicking the Crap Out of It Until It Works Properly.

AN INITIATIVE IS ONLY A START

The two most mistaken assumptions in education are extreme opposites of each other. The first is the belief that any innovation is automatically a good one. The second is the conviction that new ideas are a dangerous threat, an implicit criticism of current practice. Judicious selection of what to change, and what to leave alone, has become one of the greatest skills in managing education during a period of rapid transformation.

Anyone who wants innovations to take root must understand the nature of teaching itself. Every single day teachers engage in hundreds of interactions with their pupils. Since many of the decisions that underlie these rapid-fire exchanges have to be made in one second or less, life would be impossible without regular working habits. Deeply ingrained ways of teaching, therefore, can only be changed for the better if teachers feel some sense of ownership of the process.

I wrote a few years ago about different killer tactics that people will use towards new ideas if they feel they are being imposed against their will. One favourite is to disparage any new idea by making it look dated: 'Let me see, we tried that in 1981, 1987, again in 1993, I think. Yes, it worked quite well in 1993 . . .'

Another disabling ploy is to suggest the timing is not right: 'A bit too late for that now, isn't it?' This strategy is even more clever when the obstructionist actually appears to praise the idea. Suggesting it is ahead of its time blows the scheme into a myriad pieces, while making it sound as if the proposer is being hailed as a genius.

One of the most serious strategic errors of recent years has been to drown schools in externally imposed innovations which rarely penetrate beneath the pores of the teaching profession. They often give the impression of having been devised hundreds of miles away by some pale-faced, unrooted policy wonk in an attic, as relevant to daily life in a particular classroom as decreeing that every child should train to be a snow shoveller.

Just imagine being appointed as the government's Head of Innovation, large salary notwithstanding. It cannot be easy running an army of novelty inventors, who emerge occasionally from deep underground bunkers, blinking in the sunlight.

> 'Come in, Jenkins. Now I want to talk to you about your 2002 innovation targets. I'm afraid you're falling a bit short of what we expect.'
>
> 'A bit short, sir? What about that idea I sent you yesterday?'
>
> 'Let me see, wasn't that the plan to make teachers stand on their head when teaching about Australia? A little bizarre, I thought.'
>
> 'It's empathy, sir. That's a very "in" word nowadays in progressive education.'
>
> 'Progressive, Jenkins? We're talking about government initiatives here. Why haven't you been working on the suggestions that came out of last week's brainstorming meeting? The government is very keen on them.'
>
> 'I tried, sir, but my heart wasn't really in it. I mean, take your suggestion that children who play truant should be sold into slavery. It did seem a bit, well, backward looking.'

'Nonsense, Jenkins. We've got to take tough action. Sticking a few mothers in jail is much too flabby. This initiative will solve the truancy problem and provide much needed funds for education.'

'And I wasn't too keen on your other idea about training people to use advanced caning techniques, like the backhand flick and the forehand smash. I thought corporal punishment was banned by the European court, so it does seem very unfair on the children.'

'Children, Jenkins? Who said anything about caning children? It's the teachers I'm talking about.'

14 June 2002

Now we are all virtually real

The news that employers and universities may soon be able to tap into cyber profiles of pupils' schoolwork arouses mixed feelings. The proposal is that files containing drawings, graphics, examples of pupils' work, or recordings of their oral performance should be accessible online, as part of a national database of students' achievements.

Hmm. Time will tell whether this is a stroke of genius, a democratic means of providing instant computerised access to embryonic brilliance, or one of those slightly embarrassing 'don't ring us, we'll ring you' ideas.

On the surface the notion appears no different from external moderators scrutinising pupils' work completed during or at the end of a course. Provided that schools have ensured it is not plagiarised, or created by others, it could be seen as coursework available in electronic form, though I suspect that some pupils' text may well be proof-read and dry cleaned by a clued-up elder.

No one should forget that film and photography are art forms. The presentation of work in cyber form is not as simple a point-and-shoot assignment as it may sound. Will the finished oral or performance piece be coached or uncoached, Take 1 or Take 21, edited or unedited?

Will pupils themselves, technicians or teachers be responsible for capturing and assembling the online version available for view? If it is the responsibility of teachers then the load will be heavy. There are security and other problems if pupils have to engineer it.

Lighting, camera work, sound, editing, display can all add to or subtract from the subject. A sculpture can look different according to how well it is photographed. Give a skilful director the assignment of portraying someone's work and the result will be more impressive than an out-of-focus record produced by some bozo with a duff camera, no editing or composing skill and a twitch. Rich schools will probably sign up David Puttnam.

Even though I love playing with interactive technology I still have an eerie feeling at the thought of assessing cyber versions of humanity rather than the real thing. It may become inescapable, but it seems so bloodless.

There was once a proposal that Ofsted should conduct virtual inspections of schools. No longer would the registered inspector and chums descend with clipboard and stopwatch, trying hard to be jolly and unthreatening. Instead a distant, invisible Mr Gruesome would log on to the school's database from his remote terminal, soundlessly scouring test scores and mission statements.

It reminded me of the haunted house in Los Angeles Disneyland. In front of its entrance the three-dimensional hologram of a detached head shrieks and groans spookily inside a glass globe. Perhaps a similar cackling cyber ghoul could be placed in the entrance hall of every school receiving a virtual inspection, to remind them they were being sieved from afar. 'Heh heh heh. Welcome to special measures, dearie.'

League tables, especially of primary schools, are a good example of virtual reality. A school with a mere ten pupils taking Key Stage 2 SATs does well one year. Wonderful, an excellent place, hundred per cent at level 4 or above, top of the league. Medals, awards, status, honours duly follow.

The following cohort of ten pupils in Year 6 is not so good. Disaster. The school is now sinking, recriminations abound, the poor beggars who missed their level 4 are stigmatised, for they have let the side down. In reality the school itself is probably no different from the previous year, but the virtual version of it is now a flop.

Soon the whole of our lives could become virtual, rather than real. Fancy a meal out? Don't bother. Restaurants have all closed down, but you can look at a nice photograph of coq au vin on your computer screen and then swallow a few vitamin pills.

I occasionally meet people who have been shredded of their humanity, but the good news is that many teachers and heads have managed to retain it. Without humanity no one will even be able to tell the cyber from the actual. Virtual forms become the reality. Education already is a grand Roger Rabbit film, a surreal mixture of real people and cartoon characters.

Real or cyber?

1. Two committees are set up to look at the problems of duplication.

2. The Prime Minister's education policies are drawn up by a journalist.
3. A school with one part-time pupil receives a full-scale Ofsted inspection.
4. Two political parties bombard schools with paperwork and then both say there is too much bureaucracy.

All these are real. You and I, however, are cyber. Aaaargh! We have just completed an illegal operation and will be terminated. Log off.

17 January 2003

When did Twigg's mind snap?

What gets into intelligent people when they assume high office? Over the years I have watched some of the brightest people in the land turn into gibbering morons the minute they find themselves in a position of political authority.

One day in January, 24,000 heads of primary schools and 24,000 chairs of governing bodies opened their morning post to find a letter that left many frothing with rage. It was from junior minister Stephen Twigg, nice chap, keen, committed, salt of the earth, beat Portillo in the 1997 general election, so he earns my eternal gratitude.

Intrigued at the page full of vitriolic letters in the following week's *TES* I asked a friendly head to show me the infamous missive. 'Letter? Twigg? Can't recall that,' she said, 'but then I automatically bin anything with DfES on the top. Otherwise it melts the school's crap detector.'

Her chairman of governors had received the same message, so she retrieved a copy. I read it with mounting horror. At the end was a scrawled signature that looked like 'Sven Turge'. Was it just an embarrassed scribble, or had intelligent Stephen Twigg mutated into Sven Turge, the Nordic automaton?

Head teachers were being harangued to meet their targets. Governors were whipped into a frenzy to hobble defaulters. All schools were urged to do more phonics. What, all of them? Including those that already spent every minute of the day chanting 'ker a ter equals dog'? Presumably Sven wanted them to start an after-school activity called the 'Even More Phonics Club'. It was hard to describe these fevered missives, but the words 'blind' and 'panic' came to mind.

Next I discovered that another DfES letter had gone to chief education officers, commanding them to find out the names of every single pupil who was likely to be on the level 3/4 borderline. What on earth was going on? 'Is that Swinesville Primary? It's the CEO here. Can you read out your list for me? Right – Stan Laurel, Oliver Hardy, Morecambe and Wise, Hermann Goering, Donald Duck . . .'

As a managerial strategy this is exceptionally unintelligent behaviour. It reminds me of the stupid pheasant that walks boldly in front of my car as I drive up our road. Toot your horn and it switches direction, waddling amiably into your front bumper. It has an uncanny knack of doing the exact opposite of what it should do. If you produced a gun it would probably perch on the end of the barrel and peer down it.

I read recently about a group of scientists trying to map out the brain of a mouse. Perhaps this is too complex and they should start with an easier assignment, like mapping the brain of the simpleton who advised Sven and his mates to send out all these despairing letters, when cool professionalism is required. The message is crude and unsubtle. It reads:

> Dear Anybody
>
> There is no hope of meeting our targets, so we are absolutely bloody desperate. We haven't the foggiest idea what the hell to do. Please help us. Try anything. Get every Year 6 pupil up to level 4 by whatever means necessary. Offer large bribes, fill in their papers yourself, threaten to shoot the little buggers if all else fails, but hit those targets. And if you don't, then a van full of big blokes with broken noses and tattoos will be round in no time to break both your legs.
>
> Yours sincerely,
>
> Sven Turge

In 1993 Tim Brighouse and I worked out a means of encouraging teachers in Birmingham schools to improve by engaging them professionally in the challenge. It has been painful to observe the mangling of this notion at national level into a target-driven culture that is nothing like what we envisaged.

Targets have become a cruel master not a benign servant, focused on narrow mechanical objectives, not pupils' right to educational advantage, imposed instead of negotiated and discussed, alienating rather than engaging. As a result people develop expedient tactics, like aiming at borderliners to the cost of the majority, just to meet their targets.

The dreariness of the process is reinforced by putting the frighteners on chief education officers, so they terrorise head teachers, who are then supposed to intimidate teachers, so they in turn hammer level 3 pupils into a figure-4 shape. It is the most crass form of authoritarianism and it does not even have the virtue of being effective.

The good news is that the operation is reversible, Sven. You just shake off the fetters, as well as the cretinous minders, and turn back into intelligent Stephen. You have nothing to lose but the yoke of stupidity.

14 February 2003

three

Just testing . . .

One way of figuring out whether the education factory is producing enough sausage rolls is to apply tests. I use tests both in teaching and in my research, so I quite like them. But over the years I have also learned their limitations. It is a mistake to expect a single test to diagnose needs, sum up progress through the national curriculum, permit comparisons between schools, teachers or pupils, inform parents and employers, or tell the nation how we are doing this year compared with last year.

Unfortunately the national curriculum, and indeed the whole education system, are now tested to death. Five-year-olds are assessed on a 117-item profile. Voluntary or compulsory national tests are given almost every year of a child's life. Some 17-year-olds take five public exams in a single day. Each summer 24 million examination scripts have to be marked within three weeks, a tenfold increase within a decade or so.

Small wonder that everyone is neurotic. Heads and teachers are terrified they may drop down the league tables. Parents fret that the quality of their family's genetic capital will be questioned. Children themselves feel the stress, worried lest they in turn disappoint their parents. The nation is engulfed by tidal waves of guilt. Anxious fathers speak to unborn offspring though a tube pressed against the mother's abdomen: 'Two twos are four . . . Battle of Waterloo 1815 . . . two atoms of hydrogen and one atom of oxygen make one molecule of water . . .' Babies listen to tapes of Shakespeare in their prams.

In this hothouse atmosphere, some children can easily miss out, especially those from a working-class background. As a former member of that group, until I drew my first salary check and bought a semi, I know the traditional response to adversity. It is short, Anglo Saxon, and consists of just two words.

We all know who to blame

Did you know that adults who are seven feet tall are three feet bigger than those who are four feet high? Moreover, people who are four feet tall are three feet shorter than those who are seven feet high. There, I knew you would be shocked.

But here is the rub. When those little grown ups were babies, were they three feet shorter than the big babies? Were they hell. They were probably only about six inches shorter. So clearly they have drifted further apart as they grew – a foot shorter, then eighteen inches, two feet. Were they not eating their wheatythings properly? I blame schools.

That was more or less the reasoning portrayed in press accounts earlier this month of a report stating that differences in the performance of the best and worst schools increased as children got older. Of course they do. It would be astonishing if it were otherwise. The older, bigger or cleverer you get, the more space there is to be different. A 16-year-old with serious learning difficulties may well be performing like an 8-year-old. It is pretty hard to be eight years below average at the age of 7.

The second criticism aimed at schools was that children at the age of 7 are ahead of 'expected national standards', whereas at later stages they are behind these expected standards. The assumption seems to be that the test benchmarks originally laid down are perfect measures, therefore any deviation is a sign of failure, or success. But is it?

At a primary school in Birmingham they once entered four of their 11-year-olds for GCSE in maths. All obtained a grade C pass. In other words, using that particular thermometer, they performed like above-average 16-year-olds, five-plus years better than 'expected'.

In the Key Stage 2 national curriculum maths test, however, the same four pupils gained level 5, the supposed achievement of the average 13-year-old. On this thermometer they were a mere two years better than 'expected'.

The scores on two national tests, therefore, varied by over three years. Yet we are not talking about two different schools, two classes or two year groups. It was the same pupils in the very same month.

The identical point can be made about preliminary figures for baseline tests given to 5-year-olds on entry to school. I am in favour of the sensible use of baseline testing, having recommended it for Birmingham when I chaired their Education Commission five years ago, but only for diagnostic purposes. However, the 'norm' and 'average' merchants are already out in force.

Baseline tests are best guesses at what 5-year-old children of different abilities and backgrounds might be able to do on entering formal schooling. Many will be able to count up to ten, tie their own shoelaces. Some will be able to write their own name, and the odd one will have translated Schopenhauer into Sanskrit. Others, sadly, will display less intellectual or social skill.

As soon as it was revealed that 60 or 70 per cent of 5-year-olds could not do some of these things, the 'norm' merchants immediately began to accuse them of being 'below average' or 'failing to meet the expected standards'. At least they couldn't blame schools and teachers.

I suppose one of the biggest failures in our educational system is the large number of people who have no comprehension at all of what the term 'average' might actually mean. When the first national tests were given to 7-year-olds, roughly 50 per cent scored at level 2, the supposed 'average', and 25 per cent at each of levels 1 and 3. It was the sort of distribution you would expect.

'A quarter of pupils below average' the headlines screamed (apart from those who wrote 'a third of pupils below average'). Clearly the norm merchants will not rest until everyone is well above average, and the word itself finally explodes.

I could get to like the idea of blaming people for what is only to be expected, however. It is a really good wheeze. I must give more publicity to some little-known sins, and the villains who commit them. Did you know, for example, that:

- Most train drivers spend a third of their life fast asleep, yet they are supposed to be responsible for our safety.
- Stupid people have a much lower IQ than clever people.
- Daily newspapers must be poor, since 99 per cent of people simply throw them away, and some even use them as toilet paper.

- Thursday has never once managed to follow Tuesday; Wednesday has always got in first.
- Forty-nine per cent of all bishops are below average.

I blame schools. Might as well.

18 September 1998

A Plutonic truth is out there

In all those speculative treatises about whether aliens landed from outer space and built the pyramids at Giza, no one has yet pointed out that the working class came from Pluto. I know this for a fact, because my Uncle Ralph told me when I was a little Plutonian.

Apparently an interstellar space probe left Pluto aeons ago. On the way to Alpha Centauri someone realised there was no beer on board, so they stopped at Barnsley to try and find a pub. At that time there was no such institution and they had to move on. Unfortunately several of the pub hunters, pausing to relieve themselves behind a bush, were left behind as the starship took off.

We Plutonians have been marooned here ever since, waiting in vain for the spaceship to return, condemned in the interim to a lifetime of tin baths, chips and white sliced bread, consoled only by our whippets. Escape into the middle class, and your Plutonic origins are given away the minute you wipe your nose on your sleeve and ask for a pint pot of tea.

Our patron saint is Sisyphus, the legendary King of Corinth, whose eternal punishment in Hades was to roll a massive stone to the top of a hill and watch helplessly as it rolled back down again. Many Plutonians who have escaped from their humble roots work in public service, especially in education. The labour can sometimes seem equally fruitless, but at least you get to wear a suit.

There is permanent angst about the plight of working-class children in the education system. The facts are well established. If you are born into what nowadays are known as 'D and E households', as opposed to toffs' palaces in social groups higher up the alphabet, the odds are stacked heavily against you.

Around three-quarters of students in universities come from the two highest social groups, the As and Bs. Most of the loot in our society belongs to a relatively small percentage of the population. The bright son or daughter of a professional parent is about twice as likely to go on to higher education as the equally talented child of a manual worker.

Plutonians can find school an alienating place. When I started infant school I could never understand why, in my reading book, 'Daddy' was always taking a spade into the garden to dig. My dad sometimes worked seven twelve-hour shifts and arrived home knackered. The last thing he wanted to do was dig up the concrete in the back yard.

One multiple-choice reading test invites pupils to complete the statement 'Jimmy – – – – tea, because he was our guest'. The correct answer is 'got the best cake at', but many Plutonians choose 'washed the dishes after' and get no marks, even though they can read. It is not our fault. On Pluto you are taught that washing up is the least you can do if someone asks you for tea.

If you couldn't get your child into your favourite Plutonian school, you popped round to the chairman of governors' house and laid one on him. Here you have to put in an appeal and appear, tongue-tied, before a crowd of suits. There were no phones on Pluto either, you just shouted out of the window, which is why we are reluctant to phone the head if there's a problem.

The biggest problem on Pluto was the two conflicting forces. One pulled you away from the planet, the other held you firmly on to its surface. Education is the rocket that takes you away. Tradition is the force that holds you down. Plutonian children must be given every possible access to the rocket. That way they can choose. Remove the rocket and you eliminate choice.

Escapees are often lost. I sometimes go to quite posh places nowadays, the occasional palace even. I always wonder what I am doing there and wait for the uniformed bloke, a fellow Plutonian, to call out, 'Oi, you! Clear off!' Footballer Paul Gascoigne is marooned between his roots and the alienating Sunday supplement lifestyle that his wealth now offers him.

Deference is excruciatingly embarrassing to Plutonians, but fortunately fellow citizens rarely offer it. Years after I became an academic I bumped into a childhood friend. 'I saw thee on't telly,' he began. 'Is it true tha't a professor?' 'Er, yes,' I replied. He pondered. 'Well, bugger me.'

It was always hard to be stuck up on Pluto.

30 October 1998

Ten years of laughter and tears

Did you know that it is the tenth anniversary of the national curriculum? Although it was introduced by the 1988 Education Act, it was actually in September 1989 that 5-year-olds stepped on to the eleven-year conveyor belt for the first time. That same cohort of pioneers is just starting GCSE courses.

The story of the last decade adds a remarkable chapter to the history of education, as we moved speedily from local decision-making to the most tightly controlled central prescription in Europe. This tale of both triumph and Whitehall farce began with Kenneth Baker. Keen on publicity, he turned each report into a press jamboree: ten subjects, ten photo opportunities.

Baker's greatest wheeze was his attempt to find an explorer to chair the geography committee. Seemingly unaware that explorers tend to be out exploring, rather than sitting by the phone waiting for invitations to chair government committees, he tried in vain.

I was left with an enduring fantasy image of the great man wading neck deep up the Limpopo looking for his quarry, clad in shorts and pith helmet, hotly pursued by a television crew. It would have been marvellous to bump into him in deepest Africa and be able to say, 'Ah, Mr Baker, I presume.'

The first version of the national curriculum was farcically complex. There were seventeen attainment targets in science and fourteen in maths. The history syllabus for junior-school pupils covered all the invaders and settlers from King Ug the Caveman to the last busload of tourists, the Tudors and Stuarts, the building technology of the pyramids and Parthenon, the routes to the Spice Islands, the Aztecs, the history of plough design and plenty of others.

My favourite topic was 'The history of transport before and after the wheel', a trifle full, I always thought. History at Key Stage 2 covered over 4,000 years, allowing about one and a half minutes per year. The message was simple: avoid teaching the Spanish Armada in the hay-fever season, as someone will sneeze and the class will never know who won.

One of the biggest problems in the first phase was numerous changes, often in the same year. In January 1991 'electricity and magnetism' constituted number 11 of the seventeen science topics.

By May 1991 a reduction to five attainment targets was proposed, with good old 'electricity and magnetism' buried under the title 'forces'. September 1991 saw a further reduction to four topics. It was a game of 'Musical Attainment Targets', as dozens of topics scrambled aboard the remaining seats.

Another fiasco was the government list of great works of English literature issued to bewildered 14-year-olds one year: a single Shakespeare sonnet, a bit of Johnson's *Rasselas*, a poem about a lawn mower. Here is your official culture immunisation jab. Squish. Next

YOUR OFFICIAL CULTURE JAB

please.

Most hilarious of all were the testing arrangements for 7-year-olds. 'This is a pineapple,' teachers would say to Year 2 children in corners of crowded classrooms. 'Will it float or sink?' 'It'll float, miss.' 'How do you know?' 'It's been floating all week.'

Then there were the helpful hints from official bodies, like 'How to deal with children who are regularly absent. Test them more frequently.' But they're not actually here, sunshine. You couldn't have made it up.

There have, however, been a number of triumphs for the national curriculum, like offering entitlement for all, not just the privileged, and great improvements in science. Late 1970s inspection reports said that only one primary class in ten was getting a decent science programme, with little physical science being taught. 'Plenty of tadpoles and sticky buds, but not much electricity' was the message. Recently our pupils came sixth in the world in a large science study. There are not many areas where Britain is in the top six internationally.

So ten years of laughter and tears are now completed. I have been singing 'Happy birthday, dear national curriculum' all week to commemorate. Yet every snag encountered during those first early years was predicted before it happened. Sadly, politicians of the day ignored professional advice. It has been a salutary lesson in the folly of pursuing ideology rather than good sense.

3 September 1999

Digging holes in maths tests

The maths test set by the Teacher Training Agency for student teachers brought a tear to my eye. Good old TTA. All those 'realistic' sums based on the mathematics that teachers are supposed to know, like working out scores on tests, reminded me of sums in my childhood.

'If it takes two men four hours to dig a hole six feet square and three feet deep, how long will it take nine men to fill a bath?' Well, it was something like that. The memory plays cruel tricks after a few years.

My whole childhood seemed to be full of men digging holes and people filling up baths. I loved it. 'Realistic maths', that's what it was all about.

Indeed, you may have been wondering why every town, city and country area in the whole land has been dug up during the last year or two. Don't believe anything you read in the press about laying cable for the white-hot communications revolution. It is all lies. Not one inch of cable has ever been laid.

In fact, it is people of my generation, digging all those holes we practised so long for in our childhood. After years of withdrawal symptoms we finally broke out and decided to apply our hard-won 'realistic' maths. Me and my mates will be popping round to fill your bath some time next week.

But the interesting thing about all this 'realistic' maths was that it was only realistic on the planet Neptune. If one man can dig a hole in four hours, how long will it take two men? Two hours? No, only in maths tests. In real life it would not be so simple.

Think about it. Two men would chat to each other, swap a few jokes to while away the time, find snags, get in each other's way. They would take at least four hours, exactly the same as one man on his own. Four men would require even longer: probably write a forward plan, fill in a docket, hold a safety meeting, elect a union rep. I would say ten hours at a conservative guess.

The TTA will have to be very careful before asserting that its maths test assesses the sort of competence teachers need in their daily job. If you are an experienced teacher you are actually able to operate a kind of maths that even Einstein could never fathom, for it has its own logic and rules.

So I offer the TTA my own set of 'realistic' maths questions.

Question: If it takes a child two minutes to write one sentence, how long will it take to write ten sentences?
Answer: An hour.
Reason: That's how long the lesson lasts. All written work expands to fill the total time available.

Question: If a class of children can walk a mile in twenty minutes, how long will it take to walk the half mile from the city baths back to school?
Answer: Thirty minutes.
Reason: Darren Rowbottom will have lost his wallet and everyone will have to go back and search for it.

Question: A teacher starts marking a set of thirty books at 6 p.m. If each book takes three minutes to mark, at what time will all the books have been completed?
Answer: 7:45 next morning.
Reason: Mark ten books, watch *Eastenders*; mark four more, kids want their supper; mark another couple, kids falling out; mark five more, one little sod refuses to clean his teeth; bugger it, it's now 10 o'clock, I'm knackered; tell you what, I'll get up early and do the rest tomorrow.

Question: Sally Farnes-Barnes takes a school test where the maximum score obtainable is fifty marks. She gets ten marks in section A of the test and two marks in section B. What is her final mark?
Answer: 87 per cent.
Reason: Her dad is chairman of governors and decisions about performance-related pay are being made next week.

Only seasoned pros will get all these sums right. Nobel Prize-winning mathematicians don't stand an earthly.

18 February 2000

Busy baby has no time for hugs

Why do many parents feel they should be getting young children up to genius level? I was wondering about this when looking at some American products that involve playing videos to babies as young as a month to bathe them in Shakespeare and speeded-up Mozart.

Is it a feeling of guilt, that you are letting your offspring down if you leave the *Merchant of Venice* or the *Magic Flute* until their first birthday?

As the father of three children I remember the competitive conversations well.

'Oh yes, our Samantha was walking at ten months and knew all her letters before she even started school.'
'Really, a bit slow then was she? Our Jason could walk at nine months and was reading when he was three.'

I always wanted to join in with 'That's nothing. Our Josie was doing triple somersaults, with pike, in the womb. Then she emerged, at birth, reading Wittgenstein's *Tractatus*, singing arias from *Le nozze di Figaro* in Italian', but I never had the gall. And even if I had done so somebody would have trumped it.

The keenest 'hothousing' fans really do start in the womb. To give your offspring the best launch, you talk down a speaking tube attached to the mother's abdomen. It's true, they actually do it. I wonder what they say.

'Hello there, it's me, your mum/dad. Just a few more snippets before you pop out. Battle of Waterloo, 1815, and we beat Napoleon – that's capital N and then lower case a-p-o-l-e-o-n, by the way. Oh, and don't forget, six sevens are forty-two. Byeee. Talk to you tomorrow, when we'll be doing the eight times table and discussing John Donne and the metaphysical poets.'

I suspect that, by the time the human voice has struggled its way through the abdomen to the baby, it probably comes over as 'Flubba lubba lubba rub a dub dub', so they might as well just listen to the Teletubbies.

From one month onwards conscientious parents are supposed to be playing Shakespeare to their newly born.

'But 'tis a common proof that lowliness is young ambition's ladder . . . pay attention when I'm talking to you ... whereto the climber-upward turns his face ... look, stop breaking wind and spitting raspberry delight down your chin and listen to the greatest poet England has ever produced . . .'

One of the baby genius videotapes has syllables and odd words from various foreign languages. Listening to this is supposed to facilitate language learning in later life.

Babies do indeed reproduce all the sounds of which the human voice is capable, and some of these fade away later, through disuse, but that hardly seems a reason for playing them out of context to an uncomprehending infant. We learn our own or a second language because it is real and means something.

Imagine the situation in reverse. What good would it do to soak some hapless Russian infant in detached globs of English?' . . . shed . . . hat . . . parsley . . . hedgehog . . . ig . . . ag . . . bum . . .' I cannot see any point to it.

What are we doing to ourselves as a society when many people feel they must try to turn their infants, as soon as possible, not just into grown ups, but into adult geniuses? Is childhood itself now regarded as a luxury, a phase only permitted by parents who don't care?

There is a balance between being a conscientious parent, giving your children the best start in life, and hovering anxiously over them from birth in case they fall short of genius. Too much of the latter end of the scale may throw the delicate switch that separates curiosity from boredom.

Family games, conversations, storytelling, rolling around the floor, hugging, playing peek-a-boo, having a laugh, singing, are not just old-fashioned pastimes, they are biologically and psychologically effective ways of developing the body and the intellect.

Put the baby genius kits in the bin. The real world is much more fascinating than its synthetic equivalent.

31 March 2000

Christmas with Reg and Sid

As the festive season returns here is your special guide to everything tired teachers need for a jolly Yuletide.

SUPER CHRISTMAS GIFTS

FOR HIM
Inflatable inspector 'Reggie'
A six-foot dummy with a blow-up body and foam-rubber head. Medically proven therapeutic value. Hit it in the right place and it drones 'generally sound' in a funereal voice. Wop it again and it screeches 'below the national average' in a high-pitched whine. One more slap and its head falls off. Guaranteed hilarity all round. 'We're in special measures and I've already broken both my wrists on it' – Arthur Boggis, head teacher, Gasworks Academy.
Ofsted Inflatables Plc: de luxe model £99.99 (breaks wind noisily as head falls off), bog-standard model £29.99.

FOR HER
Inflatable supply teacher
Another winner from the same company, made in extra strong rubber, this life-sized blow-up dummy is an exact replica of a brilliant supply teacher – brim full of teaching ideas, endless patience, with huge biceps – precisely what she needs to take over her class when she is knackered. Just pull the toggle and 'Bessie' inflates instantly to teach any class any subject. 'She certainly fooled us; we thought it was the deputy head' – Year 6, Swinesville Primary School.
Ofsted Inflatables Plc: de luxe model £99.99, bog-standard model £29.99 (only says 'Copy out of your textbooks' over and over again).

FOR THE KIDS

Lunacy hour
Print your own curriculum, suitable ages 6 to 14. A set of hysterical templates allows children in your class to construct

their own silly subject and then print an impressively genuine-looking statutory order for it: 10 minutes of toenail clipping in not more than two ability groups, 15 minutes of whole-class interactive mud wrestling, 2 minutes to scratch your bum.

Initiatives Unlimited: £49.99 (with genuine recycled national curriculum ring binders, £69.99).

Game of Life

Gripping maths computer game they will play for hours. Players start at Level 1, work up to Level 8 and eventually try to gain entry to the Greatest Comprehensive School on Earth (GCSE). Stevel Knievel Byers stands in their way asking tricky questions like 7 × 8, to which the official government answer '54' must be given.

Railtrack Timefillers: £34.99.

FILMS ON TELEVISION

Carry on Leaving

Hilarious farce from the *Carry On* team with all the usual favourites. Two government agents, Sid Initiative and Ken Bulletpoint, try to get rid of all the teachers in Miss Diehard's Academy by burying them under large piles of government bureaucracy. Eventually all the teachers leave and Sid uses the school's funding to pay off his gambling debts. Meanwhile Ken goes to work for the Teacher Training Agency to dream up a few hundred more objectives and online tests and get rid of all the next generation of student teachers.

Sid Initiative	Sid James
Ken Bulletpoint	Kenneth Williams
Miss Diehard	Hattie Jacques
Sid's Bookie	Stephen Byers
TTA Official	Boris Karloff

BOOKS FOR CHRISTMAS

DfES *Little Book of Calm*

3,000 pages, 10,000 wheezes, £12.99 (post, packing and NHS truss £99).

C. Woodhead, *Life After Ofsted* (includes all *Daily Telegraph* articles)
3 pages, 29p (inc. post and packing).

CHRISTMAS HOUR

Here is the official government prescription for how all teachers must spend the hour between 12 noon and 1 p.m. on Christmas Day.

12:00 to 12:15
Access QCA website, copy out schemes of work.

12:15 to 12:30
Game of snakes and ladders, whole family, interactive.

12:30 to 12:50
Timed spelling test for individuals – must include 'accommodate', 'separate', 'discumnockeration' and 'utterbollox'.

12:50 to 1:00
Eat official Ofsted-graded Christmas lunch: two 'national average' sausages, ten 'generally sound' chips, twenty 'satisfactory' peas.

The mandatory format describing how all the other hours on Christmas Day must be spent can be found on the DfES website at: *www.stalinist/but/completely/clueless.gov.uk.*

14 December 2001

Switched off in their infancy

The possibility of infant pupils competing for a starred grade, like a national curriculum level 3★ at the age of 7, makes you wonder how far the categorisation of young children should go. Early judgements are often frail and remorseless pressure to succeed can tow in its wake the notion of failure where none exists. While some children seem to be highly competitive from birth, others recoil.

Even A-level pupils, better able to rationalise at an age when some competition becomes inescapable, can be made to feel their AAB is a dud in a finely graded system, where only top marks are seen as success. Hothoused infants may think they are incapable when they still have huge potential.

A 6-year-old boy we interviewed in a research project told us, 'I think I'm a good reader at school. I'm not a good reader at home. I can't read my books at home.' His parents were trying to push him through the children's classics they vaguely remembered reading in their own childhood, but before he was actually ready for them, so he became frustrated and demoralised.

In their early years young children desperately size up how they appear to the world. We are their mirror. Inside each of them is a delicate trip switch, metaphorical rather than real, which has an 'on' and an 'off' position. Turn it to 'off' and the vital drivers of learning soon close down – curiosity, imagination, attentiveness, the amount of time devoted to any task.

This is not an argument against challenging children intellectually, giving them stimulus, or pointing out their mistakes. It is a reason for not assigning definitive labels prematurely. Many parents and grand-parents still bear the scars of being regarded as stupid when they are not. Their trip switch was turned off, so they paid the price: a lifelong lack of confidence in their own ability to learn.

'You can't teach an old dog new tricks', 'I'm too old for computers now', 'I didn't do very well at school myself' – you hear such self-deprecating remarks from adults every day. Young children may live to be a hundred. Switch them off early and they face eighty years of aversion to new knowledge and skills after leaving school, a grim prospect. That is why I am uneasy about starred grades for twinkies. Where will this restless urge to win the infant competition end?

'My 6-year-old has just got a grade 3★ in maths.'

'Well my 4-year-old got a distinction on baseline school entry tests.'

'Mine did that at 3.'

'Really? That's nothing. My 2-year-old has read *War and Peace* twice.'

'Retarded is he? Well I can't wait for my baby to be born. She's already a marvellous pianist, passed her grade 7.'

'Pathetic! One of my husband's sperms has composed a symphony and two operas.'

I don't want to be stuffy about these things, however, so I might start my own testing agency, Opportunities to Rush Educational and Social Stigma. We at OPPRESS will provide exams for starred grades even before formal education begins, avoiding the creation of a ninny society where young children do not know their place. Our 3★ test is guaranteed to keep switches in the 'on' position.

WHERE WILL HOTHOUSING END?

Time allowed: three hours

1 Compare and contrast Tinky Winky and Dipsy as late-twentieth-century icons, commenting in particular on the semiotics of the *Teletubbies* landscape.

2 Examine the place of thiamine and riboflavin in infant breakfast cereals.

3 Goldilocks – engaging character, or thieving simpleton your grandparents think you should read about?

4 Calculate in metres the average distance covered in car journeys at the point when you ask, for the first time, 'Are we there yet?'

5 Write a critical account explaining why you insist on watching *Scooby Doo* when the villain always turns out to be the bloke who showed them round at the beginning.

6 Discuss the morality of nipping your younger sibling's arm when no one is looking (and describe some good ways of doing it).

7 Explain your parents' reasoning for weekly violin lessons, when you hate them, refuse to practise, and sound like a strangled cat.

8 Justify your action on holiday last year when you wet yourself rather than be dragged round yet another cathedral.

9 Hothousing – if you are the plant, what is the fertiliser?

10 Explain why Auntie Florence always has a dewdrop on the end of her nose.

22 March 2002

Humane rights of the tested

Such is the scale of public examinations nowadays that there have been massive difficulties recruiting enough examiners to mark national tests. Children take compulsory, and frequently the so-called 'optional' tests, virtually every single year between the ages of 5 and 18. Some exam boards have had to recruit student teachers as markers.

The clinical weighing and measuring of children by the sackload is a sad symptom of the increasingly cold relationship between the masses and their masters. Assessment has moved rapidly from the informal and intimate, to the formal and clinical. With 8 million children to be tested, almost on an annual basis, we shall soon have to hire every window cleaner, mortuary attendant and spoon polisher in the land to process the papers before Christmas.

Candidate 00439476 is known as BCBCDAC to the examination board, but his friends call him Harry. He is like Charlie Chaplin in the film *Modern Times*, frantically trying to tighten the bolt in each passing machine on the factory conveyor belt, with everything spilling remorselessly over the floor if he gets distracted.

The next wheeze to come out of the initiatives factory will be to compel every citizen to mark at least one exam paper. If you refuse, your benefits and pensions will be stopped, or you will be called up for military service. At this very moment government officials are probably standing at the entrances to supermarkets, bus, tube and train stations, offering people a few scripts to assess.

'Here you are, mark these by Friday.'
'I can't.'
'Right, you're in the army, grandad.'

Small wonder there are bog-ups in this multi-million testing industry. Finding suitable examiners must be a nightmare. A few years ago there was a mini-scandal when it was revealed that the army of Key Stage 3 examiners marking papers on Shakespeare included a postman. At least the results were delivered on time.

If Postman Pat marks the papers and then delivers them, perhaps a few more television characters could help out in the crisis. Bob the Builder can plug the gaps, while the Teletubbies could help out with baseline assessment in infant schools:

'Eh-oh, candidate 00362748.'
'Eh-oh, Tinky Winky.'

The proposal to shift national testing to computers is another symptom of the clinical view of assessment: you atomise knowledge into tiny globs and then test them one by one. This is meant to solve one problem, the shortage of examiners, but instead it creates

PASS THE SICK BAG

another, the shortage of sick bags. Anyone who thinks on-line testing is the answer should watch green-faced student teachers, on emerging from their maths and science computerised tests, head straight for the vomitorium.

The art of humanising our complex bureaucratic society is to keep it as intimate and personal as is feasible. The bigger an organisation, the more complex and distant its communications. Messages become distorted as they crawl from top to bottom of the hierarchy. Members of small groups talk to each other and sort out problems face to face, but larger groups send memos and e-mails down long chains.

Despite the convenience of e-mail I much prefer face-to-face communication. The suggestion that schools communicate with parents via e-mail should be approached with caution, especially when the message is a delicate one. It can easily appear curt and inhuman when read on a screen. There has even been a proposal that notification of a pupil's exclusion could be done by e-mail.

Gasworks Academy

-----Original Message-----

Dear Mr and Mrs Farnes Barnes

I regret to inform you that from today your son Jason is excluded from Gasworks Academy. The little wretch is now history, dead meat, persona non grata, an ex-pupil. If you call in at the school tomorrow, between 9:15 and 9:20 a.m., a security guard will escort you to his desk, where you can remove his tatty, nearly empty exercise books and his stash of chewing gum. While you're on with it, you might as well take his fleas as well. Alternatively, if you provide a fumigated box, a pest control officer will forward his miserable artefacts to you.

The importance of humane communication in a complex world reminds me of the story that used to be told back in the days when people sent telegrams for special events. On her birthday a woman was surprised and delighted to see a telegram boy arrive at the door.

'I've never had a telegram in my life,' she told him, 'would you mind singing it for me?'

'I'm afraid we don't do singing telegrams, madam,' he replied.

'Oh go on, please,' she begged.

'Very well then, just this once,' he said, clearing his throat.

'Di dum, di dum, di dum. Your Aunty Mary's dead.'

28 June 2002

Whippet fanciers still miss out

The government wants more working-class children go to university. So do I, as a former member of this disparate group of social lepers until I drew my first salary cheque and bought a semi. Children from humble backgrounds still get a raw deal in our unfair society.

There are two major problems. Recognising hidden talent is not easy. Politicians' statements suggest it is just a matter of brandishing a few 'American aptitude tests' (why are they assumed to be better than British ones?) to smoke them out from the slums. At the first sniff of these morsels of paper magic, hordes of troglodyte geniuses are supposed to emerge eagerly to claim first-class degrees three years later.

The second and related problem is that, whatever some believe to the contrary, generations of poverty and deprivation are potential killers of academic aspirations. Many working-class families fight for survival, their health ravaged by poisonous traffic fumes, living in damp and inadequate housing, or working in lousy jobs, if they have one, that pay a pittance and blight people's dignity. Identify a pupil who might benefit from higher education and there is immediate pressure on the poor beggar to grab a job if one comes up.

Previous attempts to find the Heineken intellectual test, that reaches the parts other tests cannot reach, have been disappointing. Even A-levels are modest predictors of degree class, though they are better than most alternatives.

Part of the reason is that the majority of university students will get an upper or lower second-class degree, having entered with an A, B or C grade. In other words we are using a relatively thin band of measures to predict an even thinner band of outcomes. Hence the relatively low correlations obtained.

One approach is a so-called 'culture free' or 'culture fair' test, which does not prejudice children from poor homes, but this too is difficult. Most items meant to identify potential have a cultural basis, even if this is the English language or a familiarity with concepts the disenfranchised may have missed. There is a better way. Schools should identify students with potential on the basis of their long and close association with them, so universities could then look at them seriously.

Ministers are now said to be cool on setting up an 'access regulator', the supreme watchdog who will ensure that universities recruit more working-class children. Don't believe it. I have even found a copy of the access regulator's 'culture fair' test of clever working classness. Ten out of ten on this exam and you're straight into Oxbridge.

Smart public-school toffs will probably don cloth cap and muffler and pay a fortune in private tuition fees to perfect the answers. They should remember not to blow their cover by saying, 'Ey up, old bean' in their interview.

Access Regulator's Culture-Fair Test of Clever Working Classness

Time allowed: two hours
(time and a half on Saturdays, double time on Bank Holidays and night shifts)

1. How many 10p coins will fit into a large 3 lb jam jar? How many such jars would it take to pay your top-up university fees?

2. Is keeping coins in a jam jar better than joining a Christmas club, or putting a tenner on Kemptown Boy in the 2:30 at Doncaster? Give reasons for your answer.

3. When wiping your nose on your sleeve, which part of the sleeve is likely to be least conspicuous?

4. How many peas can you balance on your knife at one go?

5. At a College dinner you are asked to say grace. Do you:
   (a) intone a piece of Latin?
   (b) say 'Bless us and these'?
   (c) recite several minutes of nonsense, so that you and your mates can grab the best food while everyone else's eyes are shut?

6. How many bags of nutty slack will fit into the average-sized tin bath?

7. How much is a full set of polyester leopardskin seat covers for a Ford Capri, if they are (a) new, (b) used, (c) on offer by a bloke in a pub as 'surplus to requirements'?

8. Either (a) draw a diagram with instructions for converting an attic or a coal shed into a pigeon loft, or (b) describe how many sheets of corrugated iron, used floorboards and six-inch nails you would need to construct your own from scratch.

9. Write an essay entitled 'Me and my six whippets'.

10. Your Aunty Doris tells you she has just been to the hairdresser, but you find her hairstyle ridiculous, what is your reply?
    (a) 'Yes, it suits you.'
    (b) 'It looks very ginger, but it'll match the cat.'
    (c) 'Were they shut?'

11 April 2003

four

Blame and shame:
teacher bashing

When things go wrong, as they are bound to in any large-scale operation like education, an immediate search is launched for handy scapegoats. According to the rules of a blame hierarchy, the shame is handed down the line until it reaches the least powerful in the chain. First in line for a good kicking are teachers and heads, though local education authorities, teacher trainers and even school inspectors may also be targeted.

In a culture where the actual operatives are thought to be the guilty party, the favoured solution is to look elsewhere, on the grounds that there must be a parallel universe of better human

beings, if only someone could find the right personality test to identify them. Another possibility is to put the system out to private companies, to offer it up to bidders in a free market. This is what happened to school inspection, when teams of freelances replaced Her Majesty's Inspectorate. Such groups are known as 'contractors', a crude term, but neat and appropriate in what has become a mechanical operation.

Unfortunately the blame culture does put off many people from applying for top jobs. Vacancies for headships attract far fewer applicants than a few years ago. Chief executives of national bodies are especially hard to find. Only the robust should step forward. Indeed, it is arguable that anyone actually applying should not be appointed, on the grounds that they cannot possibly have fully thought out what they are taking on.

The blamers are often aspiring politicians, eager to cite international comparisons, not always correctly, to persuade voters that they could do a better job of running education. One major blamer of teachers was Chris Woodhead, former chief inspector of schools. When he resigned I finally revealed the truth: I actually invented him, he was just a figment of my imagination. Sorry about that, but we satirists sometimes get desperate.

Council in a fix? Call Fastbuck

A spacecraft lands in your back garden. 'Tell me honestly,' your Martian visitor asks, pausing only to scratch the nose on the back of his cubic head with the biggest of his seven toes, as Martians do when inquisitive. 'Are human beings good or bad?'

'Well, er, it's a bit difficult,' you stammer. 'Some are good and some are bad, but it depends what you mean by "good", and er . . . ' 'Ah, you must a teacher, trying to see all points of view,' the Martian replies benignly. 'Martian teachers have the same problem when writing reports at the end of term. But are your people good or bad?'

Judging the human race as a single entity is like the current debate **LEAS: A MIXED-ABILITY GROUP** about whether local education authorities are competent or incompetent. LEAs are the biggest mixed-ability group in British education: some are excellent, some are hopeless, most are trying to do a decent job in difficult circumstances.

In any case, the very term 'local education authority' does not cover one concept. There are democratically elected politicians, professional officers, various units and departments, groups and individuals who may differ considerably in quality and competence, even within the same LEA.

The government is now advertising for a fire brigade of external consultants who can rescue a failing LEA. It is difficult to see what other options are available if the LEA has been given every chance to provide a service, but has still failed lamentably.

I would not want a local authority to be handed over entirely to a profit-making company, however. Some of the private companies' proposals for making profits, like getting rid of teachers and using educational technology instead, defy belief. 'Performance contracting', as it became known in the United States, when school districts paid private firms to teach reading, was a flop.

Part-privatisation might work, but where would the whole-hog version leave our democratic right to elect an idiot? In council elections would voters in failed LEAs be voting for local politicians or private contractors? Harry Ramsbottom, elected but clueless? Or Fastbuck Plc, imposed but rich and successful?

I am strongly tempted to reply to the government ad to become a contractor. We at Fastbuck Plc, with our Latin motto *Visas acceptamus* ('We take credit cards'), can offer failing LEAs the services of the following dream team of problem busters.

Rambo

Chairman of Education Committee a bit of a loony? Follows party line uncritically, or pursues daft political dogma? We have the solution. Rambo is your man. Brings own pump-action rifle. Little mess.

Mystic Meg

Difficulties with school admissions and parental choice? The national lottery computer generates random digits and children are assigned to schools according to how many lucky numbers they get. Mystic Meg then peers into her crystal ball and tells angry parents, 'I see a long bus journey . . .'.

Fireman Sam and Simon Spindoctor

Not getting your message across? Call in two of the senior partners of Machiavelli and Goebbels PR Consultancy to quench the flames and turn all your burned custard into crème brulée.

Regina Pre-pre

LEA not very helpful before inspections? Regina Pre-pre, fully qualified registered inspector (Dip. Insp., Hotel Eldorado, Clacton, 1994), will give schools a pre-pre-inspection. If the LEA does its own pre-inspection badly, all is not lost. By the time the real inspectors arrive the kids will have done that lesson on volcanoes three times and be word perfect.

Big Ron

Chief education officer not up to the job? Gone soft, spends all day planning to buy a cabin cruiser, or has died on the job and continued posthumously? Send for Big Ron Atkinson, saviour of many a football club faced with relegation. Free champagne and cigars provided.

Tammy Tarantula

Callers unable to get through the switchboard to the person they want? No problem. Our highly trained multi-limbed arachnid can handle eight telephones at once and also swallow troublesome visitors whole.

Bertie Bollox

Problems with bureaucracy? Need an impressive development plan or mission statement? Bertie, until his retirement a full-time writer of National Vocational Qualification documents, will craft a plan so opaque no one will know what on earth it means. ('I will springle your underpinning competencies and cost-effectively deliver your breezlebubs' – Bertie at his peak, circa 1995).

No job will be too difficult for us at Fastbuck – if the price is right.

22 January 1999

Not such duffers, after all

> 'Ladies and gentlemen of the jury, what is your verdict?'
> 'Not guilty.'
> 'I hereby sentence the accused to ten more years of hard labour
>   and regular beatings.'

Does that sound strange: not guilty, but sentenced for a crime you never committed? Isn't it what happened to Franz Kafka's main character in *The Trial*, when he was found guilty of some unexplained offence of which he was innocent, but could never obtain justice, or a proper hearing?

British teachers have been accused of producing generations of children who are the 'dunces of Europe'. Headline after headline has hammered home this very point. Apparently the Germans beat us handsomely. I have seen excellent teaching in German schools, and there is much we can learn from each other, but the real truth about standards has often been concealed.

Now Margaret Brown, professor of education at King's College, has contributed to a book, entitled *Comparing Standards Internationally*, which shows that we are not such duffers after all.

International comparisons require carefully matched samples, otherwise the findings are invalid. In some countries, for example, children are kept back for a year if they do not pass the annual assessment. This means that a class might contain none of the slower children, as they are in the year below, but include some of the lower-achieving pupils who are a year older and are thus doing the course for a second time.

In the Third International Maths and Science Study (TIMSS), one major international project looking at 13-year-olds, the German sample excluded 27 per cent of the lowest achievers, while the 17 per cent who go to special schools in Holland were omitted from their sample.

Leave out a similar percentage of our pupils and we actually beat some of the countries who are supposed to be our superiors (4–2 after extra time, the '2' are both 'own goals').

Furthermore the TIMSS test was drawn up to mirror the American syllabus, so only just over half of it actually matched our national curriculum, and Japanese 13-year-olds have spent twice as much time on maths as ours. Newspaper accounts often omit these vital facts, just as they fail to point out that we came sixth in the world in science.

Instead there is a stream of ill-informed and hostile rubbish, like the rantings of one columnist, in a poorly written piece, who confidently states that children perform badly in English because most of their teachers cannot write:'Alarmingly few of them (teachers) seem to have any ability with language because they do it so little.'

Really? I must remember to 'do' language more often. It's surely what one's mouth is for. No wonder I've always found it hard to teach when I do so little language.

Since massacring verbs is in order I may also 'eat' some music, 'kick' a bit of science and 'somersault' a few quadratic equations.

Poor old British teachers come under the cosh because we put the whole of the age group in for international tests. That's us, the

THE SUPREME INCLUDERS

supreme includers. I wouldn't want it any other way, even if we end up skewered. It does make you think, however, how history might have changed if people had only put in the right samples.

Suppose, for example, that the Russians had omitted a few soldiers at the Battle of Balaclava, then the 673 charging cavalry of the Light Brigade might have won, or at least drawn.

At the Battle of Little Bighorn if only General Custer, with his 200 soldiers, had said to Chief Sitting Bull, with his 6,000, 'Do you fancy a five-a-side?', all could have been different.

Perhaps Julius Caesar should have welcomed his unexpected visitors with, 'Nice to see you, Brutus. I'll just pop out and invite a few mates in. Then you and Cassius and your chums can play bridge against me and my seven-foot, eighteen-stone pals who also happen to own very big swords.'

You've just got to get the samples right. I must go now. I'm off to do a bit more language, as we say.

3 March 2000

More madcap memorabilia

I always thought that *Free Willy* was the title of a Hollywood film. That was until I read William Hague's speech describing what he would do with education if he became Prime Minister. Education would suddenly become free from everything, apparently, though not free from even more crackpot schemes.

The speech was nectar to those lamenting the passage of such satirical delights as Kenneth Baker-Clarke and John Patten. It was the crazy horse ideas they adopted from right-wing think tanks that sank the educational aspirations of the last Conservative government. Wee Willy Winkie would do well to treat all swivel-eyed rantings with caution.

Many of the madcap market-driven notions from the past were there, eagerly recognised by connoisseurs of Loonytunes memorabilia. Schools should be free to expand indefinitely was but one collectors' piece.

There it goes again, the elastic school. Hundreds of rubber Portakabins bounce merrily up and down the M1, having deserted shrinking establishments in quest of expanding ones. Boing, boing, boing. 'Quick, grab it!' teachers exclaim as they cluster at service stations waiting to hitch a lift on one.

Not one teacher in the land would dissent from Hague's proposal to reduce bureaucracy in schools. Unfortunately it was his own government that introduced the avalanche of box ticking and form filling that has blighted teachers' lives ever since, yet another case of the arsonists wanting credit for calling the fire brigade.

Schools should be free to pay teachers whatever salaries they wish, was another marketeers' dream turned nightmare. It would mean 24,000 heads having to negotiate 400,000 individual salary agreements every single year, or more frequently. Wonderful. That should cut down on the bureaucracy. Teachers and heads will need an agent if it ever happens. Another 10 per cent wasted on a private company.

Of course it sounds an attractive idea if sold as a means to pay teachers more, but this conveniently overlooks the fact that they may also be paid less. The market can be a useful servant, but a cruel master. 'Now, let me see, you're a single parent with two young children and there are no other schools you can teach at in this area, so we'll pay you half salary next year, take it or leave it.'

Schools can select any pupils they choose. This is a brilliant wheeze. Every school can be a grammar school. Ah, but what about those children nobody wants? No problem under Wee Willy's gormless plan, because in this chaotic rugby scrum of a system anyone can create a new school. Just set up St Dustbin's for the peasantry behind a high fence, complete with warders.

Using the sort of dubious arithmetic that might have benefited from a few numeracy hours, he abolished local authorities and produced millions of pounds extra for schools. Local democracy may have its weaknesses, but anyone who believes it is completely useless should try being one of 24,000 manila folders in some deep underground vault in Whitehall. Under Wee Willy's hapless plan we can add a few more roles to the currently crippling burden, like 'head teacher as bus driver'.

Whatever Hague may say about trusting schools rings hollow. It is lack of trust from the Conservatives, sadly carried on by New Labour, that has led not only to a huge bureaucratic load (if you don't trust people you make them write down everything and inspect them to death) but to huge stresses on teachers and heads. Now Hague wants parents to be able to call an Ofsted inspection at whim. The fundamental mistrust of teachers persists, despite the rhetoric.

It was not surprising that Chief Inspector Chris Woodhead endorsed Hague's speech enthusiastically and said it had 'struck a chord' with teachers. Hague wants even more powers for Ofsted, which strikes the sort of chord you get if you sit down heavily on a piano keyboard. He will also establish 'no notice' inspections, which means the traditional nursery rhyme will need a slight rewrite.

Wee Willy Winkie runs through the town,
Upstairs and downstairs in his night gown,
Tapping at the windows, crying through the locks,
'Ofsted are coming pal, today at nine o'clock.'

Stuff the lot of them.

21 July 2000

Let your pupils do the talking

According to a *Times Educational Supplement* news story, you can now get an online kit, for £2,000, that helps you assess your own teaching through pupil evaluations. Part of the process is to ask five pupils what they think of you. The data are then matched against national norms.

I hope people will be able to cope with the consequences. Putting oneself through the shredder always sounds like a good idea if someone else is doing it.

'What do you think of me, Jason?'
'You're crap, sir.'
'Er, thank you.'

I am in favour of sensible self-evaluation using pupil feedback as appropriate. Indeed I have just completed a series of eight books on different aspects of classroom skills in primary and secondary schools in which pupil feedback is a significant element, so I do not want to knock the idea itself. It just needs to be undertaken with caution.

'Self-confrontation', as it is known, is a delicate matter. Done well it is illuminating and will help teachers improve. Badly handled it can be psychologically devastating.

The reason is quite simple. In fields such as education, health, social work, public service, people spend their life working for the betterment of humanity. This assignment is open ended and what any individual can achieve is limited. There never is a moment when you can state that you've got it licked, nothing more to be done.

Survival in these circumstances involves persuading yourself that you are doing a decent job, otherwise you might as well hang up your boots. The problem is that too much self-satisfaction leads to complacency, too little to dismay and alienation. It is hard to strike a working balance between celebration and flagellation.

Looking in the mirror and confronting yourself is not as simple and adult as it may appear. 'Hello, ugly bugger' sounds like the grown-up thing to do if the eventual outcome is judicious self-improvement, but not if it is the vodka bottle.

As for 'matching yourself against national norms', this too appears to have a searing logic about it, on the surface at least, but national norms are insensitive to the detailed context in which people work and so may contain more image than substance. And who wants to be 'average', kept under constant temperature and pressure in a glass case, probably without air holes, as the 'British standard teacher'?

I have decided to set up a rival enterprise, offering a cheaper version than the 2,000 quid one. Just find five pupils and ask them the following questions:

- When I come into the room, does my opening remark always begin with some variation of 'Right . . .'? (national norm: 93.6 per cent)
- How often do I say 'er' in each lesson (and don't pretend you can't answer because I know you run a book on it)? (national norm: 75 times; British all-comers' record 542)
- List my three most irritating phrases (national winners: 'You can behave like that if you like, but don't expect anybody to offer you a job' and 'That's so easy my 3-year-old can do it')
- What is my most pathetic joke? (national winner: 'Has a spider written this?')
- What do you make of the remarks I write on your school report? (national norm in 1979: 'satisfactory progress'; national norm in 1999: 'Samantha is making satisfactory progress')
- What are your thoughts on the way I dress? (national norms: 'Just like my grandma/grandad' 58 per cent; 'We particularly admire your Hush Puppies' 26 per cent; 'I too support the local Oxfam shop whenever possible' 11 per cent; 'Nice elbow patches' 5 per cent)
- What are my interpersonal relationships with pupils like? (national norm: 'We call you Genghis')
- How often do I mark your homework? (national norms: 'Termly' 14 per cent; 'Weekly' 12 per cent; 'Weakly' 10 per cent; 'What homework?' 64 per cent)
- How do I distribute my time? (national norms: 'You manage to get round everybody to check on progress' 28 per cent; 'Crawling to the head to get a performance bonus' 72 per cent)
- Is there anything I can do to improve your learning? (national norms: 'Legalise morphine' 86 per cent; 'Turn up' 14 per cent)

Send a mere fiver and we at *www.money-for-old-rope.co.uk* will offer a complete pupil feedback kit for every occasion.

20 October 2000

Woodhead was my sick joke

'Alas, poor Woodhead! — I knew him, Horatio: a fellow of infinite jest, of most excellent fancy.'

Given the lucrative jobs he will be taking up, the word 'poor' seems inappropriate. But I want to confess something.

I invented Chris Woodhead. There, I've said it. I apologise if I upset anyone in the process. We satirists can sometimes get desperate, so one day I made him up. Reprehensible, I admit, but I was young and silly. He was, so to speak, my Piltdown Man.

The idea was meant to be so transparent everyone would recognise it was a spoof. The ultra-progressive teacher, teacher trainer and LEA administrator turns into a traditionalist, scourging teachers, teacher trainers and LEA administrators.

Easily bored, he went on, in my storyline, to write for a Conservative newspaper, become a consultant to a Conservative PR firm and then a Conservative peer, Screaming Lord Woodhead. Incredible, I thought, no one will fall for it.

Even the name was a clue. Unsure whether to call him Chris Smartguy or Sid Turniphead, I settled on a compromise. I thought I had overdone things sufficiently for everyone to rumble, but somehow he just grew in my fevered imagination until people assumed he was real.

The hardest moment came when I had to take part in a debate with him at the London Institute. Talking sense one minute and bollocks the next, running up and down the stage so fast that no one

INSPECTION HELD PROGRESS BACK

noticed there was only one of us, was absolutely knackering, but I must have fooled those present, since I beat myself by 900 votes to 25.

And posing for all those photo opportunities, dripping with gravitas, sometimes wearing climbing gear and severe spectacles while dangling from a cliff, was absolute murder, I can tell you.

I still find it difficult to separate fantasy from reality. Since he took on a life of his own the fantasies have proliferated in the right-wing press. To make up for what I have wrought I want to disarm some of them.

Myth number one is that he raised achievement. In truth, standards rose despite Woodhead, not because of him. Scores in GCSE and A level improved for years before he ever appeared. Philip Hunter, chief education officer of Staffordshire, showed that standards rose faster in schools that had not had an Ofsted inspection than in those that had. The retro-rocket of inspection held progress back.

Myth number two is that he had to act tough. Yet it was a survey by old-style HMI, revealing that only one primary class in ten was getting a decent science education, that led to a huge collaborative effort. We are now sixth in the world in science: no bluster, no scourging, no headlines, no Woodhead.

Myth number three is that he was a lone courageous battler against a teaching force unwilling to improve. We all know the odd teacher who has ground to a halt, but every year most of the 400,000 teachers in the land run their socks off, one of the most stressed of professions. No one came into teaching to lower standards, so why was it ever assumed that he had sole lien on virtue?

Myth number four is that he alone organised Ofsted to inspect all 24,000 schools. This ignores the huge contribution of Mike Tomlinson, Anthea Millett and Jim Rose, senior inspectors who achieved the near impossible.

So what will the reality be in future? According to press accounts 'Friends of Woodhead' (come again?) say that his literary masterpieces will lambast Labour next March. So it's no more Mr Nice Guy. After his huge pay rise and loyal support, the word 'gratitude' seems to be missing here.

There are so many ironies: the critic of media studies now a media employee; the courtier of journalists who becomes one himself; the PR consultant whose public relations with teachers were less than brilliant. Was he really a figment of my imagination? I am past knowing.

I have begun to pen my/his devastating memoirs: 'Went into the office, hammered the teaching profession, went home, climbed up mountain, climbed back down again, played with train set.' Alas, like him I'm bored already.

17 November 2000

Only the constipated need apply

A man was once taking a personality test. He looked long and hard at the question on the paper in front of him. It asked 'Are you decisive?' He chewed on his pen, agonised for some time, made as if to write his answer, but then drew back. Eventually, after much angst, he circled the word 'Yes'.

The belief that human behaviour and characteristics can be measured with great precision has become pervasive. There is pressure for those seeking senior posts in education to be subjected to personality testing, as if this would avoid future problems. It would not and it might even create a few.

I have used personality testing in my own research in a strictly limited context and I would certainly not make it the basis for something as important as a senior appointment. Advocates of pencil-and-paper personality tests usually fail to tell you of their considerable limitations. For a start there is what is called 'function fluctuation': we can be different people on different occasions, tough in some situations, tender in others.

The predictive power of personality scores is not as high as is claimed and is confounded by such matters as intelligence. Clever people can fake answers and may succeed because they are smart, or devious, not because they possess the qualities the test purports to measure. No they can't, say the test fans, we spot fakers through items that detect 'motivational distortion' – what peasants like you and me call 'fibbing'.

Well can they? These items include such masterpieces as 'Was your mother always a good woman?' (wow, that really fooled me) and, I kid you not, 'Often my bowels don't move for several days at a time', disagreement with which is supposed to indicate you are lying. So some poor bastard who munches prunes and bran for breakfast every day, and is telling the truth, will never get a headship. Do anyone's bowels actually stay still, incidentally, i.e. remain in the chair after they have got up and left? I think not.

When I see garbage like this I want to make up my own items, like 'I always spread strawberry jam on my sausages', or 'I never hiccup when I vacuum a carpet'. They would probably have as much predictive power as the real thing.

While sensible advocates admit the limitations of written tests, the zealot end of the spectrum sees no problem, but then peddling such wares is a lot more lucrative than selling snake oil. Worse, some users are completely clueless about what underlies personality testing.

I was once on an interviewing committee for a senior post, so I asked the representative of the headhunting firm, gleefully parading his bag of baubles before the panel, to tell me about the test's norms and principles. If I could have photographed his face I would have put it on my Christmas cards. I cannot reveal which appointment it was, but I can tell you that this particular witch doctor's predictions were spectacularly wrong.

Human testing of other kinds is much more valid and reliable, but still has its limitations. More effort has been put into the testing of intelligence during the last eighty years than into most aspects of human competence and a great deal of the work is brilliant. Yet verbal IQ scores, for example, tell us only a limited amount about educational achievement, because there are many forms and features of intelligent behaviour, often unmeasured, which show low correlations with verbal IQ.

I would not make applicants for senior posts in education take written personality tests, with or without the bowel questions. They should only be used, if at all, around the edges, for background information. No one wants a constipated head teacher or chief education officer (whispering into someone's ear 'Ofsted are coming next week', incidentally, has never been known to fail), but a thorough assessment of track record and potential is a better bet than a test score founded on sand.

In future, if anyone refuses to acknowledge the limitations of written personality tests in my presence, I shall suggest they insert them in the very fundamental orifice with which their fib-detector item seems so concerned.

2 November 2001

Go on, have a shot at exam job

Psssst! Fancy an important job? Couple of days a week, bus fares provided, a bit of spending money? After all the fuss over A levels, and the sudden departure of Bill Stubbs as chairman of the Qualifications and Curriculum Authority, it makes you wonder who might be willing to take such high-profile public-service jobs in future.

The time is long past when people who were successful in their field assumed that one day, later in their career, they might make a significant contribution to education by taking on a leadership role in a great national body. Nowadays these jobs, especially if they are in sensitive areas like examinations or curriculum, are about as desirable as a swim in a crocodile-infested swamp.

Consider some of the pitfalls. First of all you know that any mishap, major or minor, will lead to a monumental fuss in the press. There will be some good and accurate accounts, but there will also be reporters who display the worst traits of their profession, purveying lies, fantasy, ignorance.

The great hypocrisy of the A-level grading fuss was that some of the politicians and journalists who made the most pious statements about children being 'robbed' of their A grades, would have been even more incandescent if they had actually got them. Standards, they would have screamed, had now fallen to subterranean levels and the end of the world was nigh.

So what else is there to look forward to if you take one of these high-profile public-service jobs? You will have to watch every word you utter, for a start. Forget any lighthearted spontaneous remarks, they will simply be taken out of context and used to smear you. Comment cheerfully on the fine weather one sunny morning and the headline 'Exams boss smiles as standards plummet' will inevitably follow.

Another hazard is that you will be briefed against by spin doctors the moment anything goes awry. Ronnie Rottweiler or some other invisible spinner will ring round the press telling them that it is entirely your fault and the skids are under you. When you finally get the bullet your only consolation is that

MORE SPINNED AGAINST THAN SPINNING

you will be more spinned against than spinning.

Still want a high-profile public-service job? If so, try responding to these key interview teasers.

Question 1: A new version is launched of an existing examination, which, for the sake of argument, we will call A level. Imagine you are the regulator of the examination boards. Do you (a) say something to them about the standards of the new version compared with the previous form, or (b) say nothing to them about comparative standards?

If your answer is (b) and you would say nothing, then you are fired already. How on earth can we hire you as a regulator when you do not say a single word about the relationship of the new version of the exam to the old? So your answer must be (a) if you are to survive to the next part of the inquisition.

Question 2: What do you actually say to the exam boards about the standards of the new exam compared with the earlier version? Do you say (a) the standards required to obtain each grade should be about the same as previously, (b) the standards of the new exam should be lower, (c) the standards of the new exam should be higher, or (d) do you sing 'Oh I do like to be beside the seaside'?

You would be vaporised if you told exam boards to make standards either higher or lower, and Bill Stubbs was fired for telling them they must be about the same, so that clearly rules out answers (a), (b) and (c). The only acceptable response is to sing a lusty chorus of 'Oh I do like to be beside the seaside'. That way you will be seen as an engaging eccentric, likely to get away with murder.

There is only one profession, so far as I can see, that can possibly provide suitable candidates for major public-service jobs in education in future and that is football management. After all, football managers have got everything it takes: they have already received their share of bullshit from the press and they are constantly being fired, usually after a vote of confidence from their directors.

The solution, therefore, is simple. There should be no more angst about who will be sufficiently talented and robust. The next chairman of the QCA must be a football manager with a sense of humour. The best candidate is obvious: former Derby County and Nottingham Forest maestro Brian Clough. I rest my case.

11 October 2002

Are you a flapper or a fighter?

The most senior jobs in education are beginning to look increasingly undoable in the present climate. Anyone who has been in education for a few years knows that a problem can blow up at any time, even in the best-run schools. For years such hiccups were resolved locally, with little fuss. Since education became a high-stakes policy area any disturbance of the norm is seen as a national tragedy, a potential front-page headline.

With 8 million children and 400,000 teachers in 24,000 primary and secondary schools, there are bound to be incidents on a daily basis. From time to time during the school year a pupil will get into a rage, a parent will remonstrate, a teacher will burn out, a head will spread marmalade on national test papers or turn up to assembly in a Batman outfit. The more pathetic of our journalists and politicians will then portray the abnormal as the normal.

Before long a well-rehearsed ritual swings into action. Local and national reporters doorstep the school, screwing quotes out of anyone, authoritative or not. The BBC programme *Panorama* hired a massive crane to shoot film directly through windows of the troubled Ridings School, with no indication of the context of what was being shown, beyond speculation.

Individual head teachers, people like Bill Stubbs who chair national organisations, even the Secretary of State herself, are persecuted, or hounded out of their jobs. A few years ago Bob Salisbury, a Nottingham head, was vilified by the tabloids for accepting restaurant vouchers, so that pupils who had done well in work or attendance could take their parents out for a meal.

It was probably the only way these not especially wealthy pupils could give their family a treat, but the head was wrongly accused of offering them booze, because the meal would have been in a perfectly respectable chain of pub restaurants. Yet they would have been expressly forbidden to consume alcohol. Fortunately Bob had the last laugh when he was knighted.

People are normally selected for senior posts on the basis of their professional competence, not their ability to cope with lies and fabrications. Perhaps this now needs to change, so I have devised a new personality test, called Screening Out Deficient Or Feeble

Flappers, specially designed to identify the tough-minded. SODOFF is guaranteed to find those robust characters who can cheerfully taken on a senior post and then weather the inevitable storms.

1 **During a parents' evening a teacher in your school says to a father 'Bog off, you thick git'. Do you:**
   (a) say to the parent 'He's a laugh, isn't he?'
   (b) crawl
   (c) congratulate the teacher on his discernment?

2 **A journalist rings up to say that some of your pupils are selling drugs outside the school gate. Do you:**
   (a) say 'I hope they're not undercutting the tuckshop'
   (b) promise to use rack and thumbscrews on the offenders
   (c) calculate how many teachers' bonus payments could be funded by a percentage of the takings?

3 **An Ofsted inspection team tells you that the school is likely to be put into special measures. Do you say:**
   (a) 'Special measures? You mean pints and gallons, that sort of thing?'
   (b) 'I may not be back for some time', and then turn on your heel and plummet head first from the top of the school
   (c) 'Is that bloke Woodhead still with you? Decent sort, I always thought'?

4 **Five teachers threaten to resign unless a key vacant post is filled soon. Do you:**
   (a) tell them that, as there is no money left in the budget, a whip round will be necessary and a grand each should do it
   (b) burst into tears and offer to teach the programme yourself
   (c) say 'A vacant post in your department? I wonder anyone noticed'?

5 **A pupil burns the school down one night. Do you:**
   (a) ask staff if there are any government lesson plans and tickbox sheets they would like to add to the pyre

    (b) rush to assist the firefighters, even offering to piddle on
         the blaze if no spare hosepipes are available

    (c) put the pupil forward for a citizenship award and invite
         him to open the new building?

If your answers are:

mainly (a) – you have a nice mixture of humour and naivety and will go far

mainly (b) – your eagerness to please blocks any chance of preferment in modern education

mainly (c) – congratulations, you could cynic for England, so welcome to the headship of Gradgrind Academy.

8 November 2002

Lay down your prescriptions

A most unusual letter from a head teacher arrived in the morning post. Would I mind, it asked, leading a revolution? Heads and teachers were in utter despair about barmy prescriptions. Someone was needed to lead a revolution, so could I kindly start one? Thousands would follow.

As a fully paid-up member of Apathetics Anonymous (if ever you think of rebelling, someone rings you up and talks you out of it) I was shaken to the very centre of the string of jelly I call my spine. We buttock-clenching British professionals don't do revolution.

Stamp your foot and say 'Drat!', put an official letter through the shredder, cry into your cocoa, stage a decent collective whinge, all these are fine. But revolution is strictly for the French.

The first and last time I started a rebellion was at the age of 12. We boy-scout members of the peewit patrol awoke one morning in summer camp to find that our flag had been stolen during the night. Full of revolutionary fervour I proposed that we storm the tent of the older boys who had nicked it. Everyone agreed. A firm strike at our arrogant seniors was the only answer.

I wondered why the mischievous thieves were doubled up with laughter as I approached the whites of their eyes, bellowing 'Charge!' at the top of my voice. It was because my five patrol mates, erstwhile fellow revolutionaries, were by now disappearing over the horizon in the opposite direction twice as fast as I was running at the enemy.

Like most people in education I really wanted to believe the government's hint that the days of prescription were over, that 'weapons of mass instruction' were banished for ever. The unhappy truth became apparent during and after Christmas in a welter of announcements.

Teachers in primary schools would be required to do yet more phonics; heads and governors were harangued to meet their targets. We must have more tractors, even if they are piled up in the back yard.

It would not be so bad if telling teachers what to do actually worked, but it doesn't, as schools in Wales have demonstrated by improving numeracy and literacy faster than in England, without the heavy hand of government. The key ingredient, trust of profes-sionals, is simply missing.

Instead a fundamental suspicion, virtually impossible to displace, decrees that every move must be determined from the centre. Teachers' judgement is out, they themselves are emasculated.

Without an appeal to individual imagination and creativity how are we going to recruit the 200,000-plus new recruits needed over the next decade, as masses of seasoned practitioners hang up their chalk? Who will want to be a mere technician with a stick of chalk, waiting for the next set of instructions to arrive in the post? Certainly no one with spirit.

Contempt can be a major provocation of revolution. There is no exact equivalent of a Hippocratic oath for teachers, but it is only loyalty to children, parents and the community that has prevented mayhem in the last few years. Stiff upper lips abound, hands are liberally wrung, but no one wants to jeopardise children's one chance of a decent education.

Saddam Hussein was set targets, as is appropriate in this target-mad world, so I am putting forward a last possible condition for achieving the full disarmament of further barmy, unrooted proposals. There are six tests that must be met. The actual wording remains under discussion, but the essential requirements are:

1   a public statement, in English, by the Prime Minister admitting to the possession and concealment of prescriptions of mass destruction and declaring his regime's intention to give them up
2   a number of members of the Number 10 policy unit (probably about thirty) to be allowed to go abroad, together with their spin doctors, for interview
3   the surrender of any hidden prescriptions and other bureaucratic initiatives, or an explanation of their previous destruction
4   an explanation of the drone found cowering in the DfES by inspectors, together with the numbers and locations of any others
5   a commitment that the so-called 'mobile initiatives', like the 117-item checklist for 5-year-olds and prohibitive top-up fees for students, will be surrendered for destruction
6   a commitment to the destruction of 'prescribed missiles', including the remaining proposals of Ad-Onis, but possibly others also.

I may be prepared to drop the first requirement, as very few education initiatives have ever been expressed in English that anyone understood, but if the government does not comply, then I shall reconvene the peewit patrol and revolution will follow. Provided that's OK with the Number 10 policy unit, of course.

28 March 2003

five

Inside the classroom

What rescues education from complete calamity is, in the end, the teachers and heads who do their job well. At the beginning of the twenty-first century two-thirds of teachers were over 40, so it was a very experienced profession. Replacing them, however, has become a major headache. Potential recruits know that it is a stressful job and from time to time they will be reviled, or ridiculed in television programmes. Meanwhile old hands are hanging up their chalk early.

Yet teaching itself remains as fascinating and rewarding as it has ever been. It is what goes with it, the penumbra of box ticking, form filling and irksome bureaucracy, that is odious. Then there is the

increased risk nowadays of being sued for accidents on field trips, or vilified for teaching controversial subjects like sex education, a subject I would only teach by putting on a video and running out of the room, the 'withdrawal method'.

Life in a classroom is exceptionally busy. Teachers may engage in 1,000 or more exchanges in a single day. Many teachers will have asked a million questions in their first fifteen years of teaching. They know the answers to most of them and people have been locked up for less. They will make most of their routine decisions in one second or less, an astonishing human feat, given the complexity of human interaction. It should not be a profession that is abused.

Primary teachers and heads in particular have lost confidence in their own professional ability. Many are too scared to do anything other than what is prescribed, petrified even of undertaking time-honoured 'projects', though there are signs that these may make a long-overdue return. Head teachers are even offered 'leadership grants' which they may use to sack themselves, despite the difficulty of recruiting replacements. It's a mad world.

Stray teachers in the doghouse

I used to think that being over 50 was a rotten idea, but now it seems rather a good thing. The coming decade will be the golden age of the fiftysomethings in teaching. As a consequence of the high rate of recruitment in the 1960s and 1970s, the current estimate is that in 2006 about half of all men teachers and 40 per cent of women teachers will be over 50.

Fears that the nation's teachers will inevitably become knackered has-beens are exaggerated, however. Teaching is a profession in which experience can be a handicap or a blessing. Every year teachers engage in about 200,000 exchanges with pupils – questions asked, praise given, reprimands, information swapped. That adds up to about a million transactions every five years of your career.

As a result people either close their minds, believing they have mastered their craft, or carry on learning, capitalising on their enormous experience to make judicious changes to what they do. It is a job you can get better and better at, provided you have not switched off your imagination and zeal. The message is clear: use it, or lose it.

The psycho-analyst Erik Erikson described middle age as a struggle between 'generativity', the ability to do something for the next generation, and 'stagnation', increasing personal impover-ishment. If generativity wins, then the nightmare of deadbeat staffrooms in 2006 is groundless. Far from being an army of elderly Viagra-crunchers with artificial hip joints, teachers could be at the height of their professional powers.

What is less exciting is the prospect of trying to recruit enough newcomers. Around 150,000 new teachers will be needed in the decade 2006 to 2016, to replace those retiring. One **USE IT OR** possible strategy is to winkle out some of those **LOSE IT** escapees who quit the profession and persuade them back in. If you leave teaching prematurely, you become part of what is officially known as the PIT, the 'Pool of Inactive Teachers'.

I was reminded of the existence of this substantial cavity by a letter from a teacher suggesting that the teacher shortage could be resolved at a stroke if we used the strategies of the dogs' home for rounding up strays. Brilliant. I suggest we turn the Teacher Training Agency into the Bonzo Recruitment Agency. Each agent will be given a large net and a low-pitched whistle (so that older ex-teachers with a hearing loss can hear it).

A large 'teacher pound' will be set up on the outskirts of major towns. Any stray ex-teachers rounded up can be kept behind secure wire fences, howling away under a large caption saying 'Remember: a teacher isn't just for Christmas', as they wait for a desperate head looking for someone to teach maths.

Individual cages will also allow customers to hand pick a teacher for a particular purpose: solemn-looking Bassett-hound types to replace the staffroom cynic; sleek sheepdogs for playground duty and escorting field trips; frisky terriers to worry away at problems until they are solved. If there are insoluble crises, recruits from Bonzo can always cock a leg at them.

Senior teachers can be collected from a special pound, looked after by an agent known as 'Deputy Dawg'. If you want a deputy head responsible for pastoral care, I recommend our Alsatian type, obedient, solicitous, but with teeth when needed. We can supply the occasional Rottweiler, but only under licence.

Head teachers looking for teachers who are utterly compliant will like our selection of poodles and lapdogs. If you want someone determined, able to collect in test scores and exam marks assiduously, badgering teachers who fail to return them on time, then I can recommend one of our many bulldogs.

Should your need be more for someone to fizz around chasing every trendy new idea, choose one of our whippets. If you require a teacher who is willing to run round in circles for no purpose what-soever, our greyhounds would be ideal. Free mechanical hare supplied.

All our recruits will normally be indistinguishable from other teachers in the school. Should you want to know whether a Bonzo Agency teacher is in your midst, however, there is one big giveaway. If you whistle, their ears prick up and they come rushing over to you, panting. Unless that's the head on Viagra.

5 March 1999

The fine art of bluffication

If esteem in our society were based on skill with a paintbrush, then I would be a leper. I love paintings, but cannot do them. My heart sank whenever teachers said, 'Now draw a picture of it.' My effort to depict a horse would be an insult to a camel. I once tried to draw a feather for my daughter and she thought it was a sausage.

The problem is that I was never actually taught to paint. There seemed to be an assumption, in the school I attended, that art was worth one lesson a week. If clever children were left to splosh paint on to paper, it would be good therapy and a nice rest.

A very good art graduate in my university tutorial group once encouraged us to use our eyes properly and think about what we were trying to depict, showed us how to hold a brush, mix colours. Before long most of us did the best artwork of our lives.

I would also be a pariah if spatial intelligence were at a premium. Several members of my family are geographically dyslexic. We are the exact opposite of homing pigeons. If we emerge from a hotel room and turn left, the lifts and reception must be to the right. 'Homeless pigeons' is more accurate. I consciously map where I have parked the car, otherwise I would still be touring the streets at midnight. When they were doling out the lodestone, our genes were at the back of the queue.

There are many kinds of intelligence to be found among children and adults and, with help and stimulus, these can develop. When mental testing was first introduced, it was often assumed there was a single fixed form of intelligence, incapable of change, but this was soon shown to be mistaken.

The psychologist Charles Spearman proposed a two-factor theory, arguing that there was 'g', a general intelligence factor, and 's', specific mental skill in fields like mathematics or science. Subsequently J. P. Guilford developed a multidimensional model of intelligence, as did Howard Gardner more recently.

Think of the intellectual effort needed to work out on paper how much and what angle of force to apply to a ball to make it land on a precise spot 40 metres away. The weight and shape of the ball, the wind speed and direction, the parabola of flight would all have to be taken into account. Several hours, or even days might be needed. Yet professional sports players will apply just the right force in a split second.

Although schools are better now at recognising different talents, there is still reluctance in society to value intelligence outside restricted areas. Language intelligence is especially esteemed nowadays in our communication-rich society, as it should be, but even mathematical expertise is sometimes seen as quirky and oddball.

If the full richness of human competence is to be recognised, there are ten modern areas of professional intelligence that are still relatively unsung among teachers.

1. *Busibility* – managing to look busy, as if the problems of the world lie heavily on your shoulders, particularly when asked to fill in for an absent teacher.
2. *Bluffication* – the capacity to look more expert than you are, for example, using the term 'information and communication technologies' when you don't actually know how to switch on a single machine.
3. *Creepescence* – knowing when and to whom to grovel.
4. *Quitology* – choosing the right moment to call it a day.
5. *Queuesense* – the ability to pick the fastest-moving queue in the supermarket or select the quickest route to promotion.
6. *Bandwagonery* - knowing when the wheel is about to come off the bandwagon you are on and which new one to leap aboard.
7. *Teflonism* - cleverly evading responsibility for bog-ups, or slipping blame on to a colleague.
8. *Somnia* – boring a class in a soothing manner, without provoking a riot.
9. *SATuration* – getting good test scores from pupils, despite not having taught them anything.
10. *Bakerspeech* – fluent use of post-1988 jargon, like 'deliver the curriculum', without ever blushing or realising that it has rotted your brain.

30 April 1999

Saying 'no' to unprotected sex

The news that Britain has more teenage pregnancies than many other countries was accompanied by the sensible suggestion that education can play an important part in addressing the problem. Ignorance exacts a heavy price in our society and it is a pity that so many lessons are learned only after a disaster has occurred.

What was unfair, however, was the direct and implied criticism of schools in some press coverage. During the past two decades in particular there has been complete apoplexy in certain quarters every time sex education was mentioned, so it is a bit hypocritical to blame schools for not doing something that many powerful people were eager to suppress.

My generation received no official sex education. We had to make sense of muttered bike-shed conversations with older, but sadly not wiser, pupils or try to guess the relevance of the odd biology lesson on 'reproduction'.

In the early years of secondary school most of us only learned about the amoeba and something called 'binary fission'. Convinced that we would one day split in two and create a clone containing half our contractile vacuole, protoplasm and ectoplasm, whatever they were, it was no wonder that we could never understand why grown-ups became so excited about sex.

To this day few of my generation can face teaching sex education classes. I personally will not go near the topic, though I am full of admiration for those who can coolly slide a condom over a banana in front of the acne brigade without their face turning the colour of tomato ketchup.

The last government was so edgy about sex education that it banned local authorities from playing any part in it. Shortly after-wards the Aids crisis occurred and the very same government then asked LEAs to spearhead a campaign, having just removed their powers to take action. It was typical of the hypocrisy and hysteria that have surrounded the issue.

Indeed, given the bedlam generated over sex education in the past, it is not surprising that head teachers have been extremely wary of how the subject was tackled. A few years ago I interviewed a number of heads about how they used school broadcasts. Many were grateful that the BBC produced a sex education series, as they felt it offered some protection to be able to say they were following the same programmes as thousands of other schools.

Yet some heads told a different story. In one school they had to use an earlier BBC series, because the newer programmes covered Aids and some parents had vetoed this even being discussed.

Another head had been prevented from tackling the topic because a local politician insisted that children would immediately go out and practise what they had learned, something which never happened in the case of the school's modern language lessons.

A student teacher, about to cover the agreed sex-education programme in the school where she was doing her practice, sensibly asked the class to write down their questions, so she could discuss with the head of department how to deal with the matters raised. When he read the questions through, the head of department split them into two piles, labelled 'yes' and 'no'. The taboo topics mainly involved the region of the body situated between the waist and the thigh, roughly the area covered by a pair of shorts. Since amoebas don't wear Bermudas, we never had that sort of problem when I was at school.

Society must now make up its mind. Do we want children to receive sex-education classes at school? If so, then teachers who try to teach the topic in a sensitive, informative and thoughtful way must not be pilloried. If we don't, then any blame for unwanted pregnancies or increased promiscuity should not be laid at the door of the schools.

My own position has always been clear. If compelled to teach sex education I shall either put on a video and sprint out of the room (the withdrawal method), play a ghetto blaster at full volume so nobody can hear a word I am saying (the rhythm method), or lecture with a bag over my head (the sheath method).

25 June 1999

Those chimps aren't so clever

Guilt, that's what it is, pure guilt. No, don't deny it, that's the worst thing you can do. Just admit it, you curmudgeonly failure, you substandard piece of yak dung. Like me you are guilty as charged. You and I have let down the whole human race. Woe is us, alas, alack . . .

Oops, sorry about that. Only I have been trying to work out why I feel a stab of guilt, a sweat of remorse, or whatever the term is, every time I read about yet another supposed failure by the nation's children. Kids simply ain't what they used to be.

Did you know that chimpanzees can count as well as children? It's a fact, because it said so in the papers. A group of chimps were able to count up as accurately as primary pupils. Damn. Another failure by the teaching profession, unless of course they had been moon-lighting with the chimps down at the local zoo to supplement their meagre income.

So much for the numeracy hour, I thought, until I realised that the report had come from Japan. What a relief. Japanese teachers will now probably get the same stick as British teachers.

On the other hand, perhaps chimps are super clever in the Far East. Maybe they sit in rows chanting their tables, while avid western observers sit and watch open mouthed, scarcely able to contain their excitement at the novelty of witnessing whole-class interactive teaching.

This was only the latest in a long catalogue of failure by teachers and parents, locked together in their collective guilt. There was another ill-tempered attack on the poor beggars charged with bringing up the next generation a few weeks ago. 'Children don't even know where their food comes from', some pundit thundered angrily in a newspaper interview.

Yes they do. It comes from Sainsbury's. They are very smart shoppers. I see them in there with their parents on Sunday mornings grabbing the last double pack of bacon with the 200 extra bonus points.

'Get off you little sod, I saw it first.'
'Dad, that man's trying to nick our air miles.'

I once went to a Council of Europe meeting at which MPs from all over Europe lamented the ignorance of their nation's youth. 'Do you know,' the man from Switzerland thundered, neck puce with rage, 'children in my country can't even tell apple blossom from cherry blossom nowadays?' Collective shock rippled around the chamber as the continent's democratically elected representatives tried hero- ically to simulate rage at this utterly meaningless indignation.

But, to return to the guilt trip, the issue was made clearer for me by the psychoanalyst Erik Erikson. He described eight stages in human development, each of which was accompanied by a potential crisis. The stage that many teachers and parents are in is the phase of 'middle adulthood' when the tension is between 'generativity' and 'stagnation'. For Erikson 'generativity' involves mentoring the next generation, hence the sense of guilt in middle age if you are accused of failing.

The retired generation of golden oldies in our society is seen as gritty and resourceful: surviving the war; for ever making nutritious soups and stews out of a carrot, a marrowbone and a pair of old socks; singing 'Roll out the barrel' defiantly in cellars and tube stations, while flying bombs whistled overhead.

I once saw my 92-year-old great aunt running for a bus and missing it, two heavy bags in her hands. When she had finished shouting a mouthful of abuse at the departing bus driver, I asked her why she was so angry. 'I do the shopping for the old folks,' she said, 'and they'll get upset if I'm late back.' It makes you sick.

We middle-aged wimps are thus caught in between envy of these elderly superheroes and our futile attempts to bring up younger generations that regard us as old-fashioned fogies, longing for our flares and round-toed sandals. Every perceived failure cuts us to the quick.

But if chimps are so bloody clever then perhaps they should be solving the teacher recruitment crisis. After all, if you pay peanuts you get monkeys.

21 January 2000

Time to rat on TV's teacher prat

Why do so many television portrayals and films about teachers get it wrong? I watched the first programme in the new Channel 4 series

HELLO P45 *Teachers* in eager anticipation, but found the central character (a 'call me Simon' teacher) to be a monumental prat. I ended up wanting to hurl my boot through the television screen at him and then chuck the set under a passing juggernaut.

Within the first episode he had managed to do several things that would have had a real teacher up on a disciplinary charge. He talks to a class of pupils about their sexual fantasies, and when one girl mentions she likes the footballer Ryan Giggs, he writes up on the blackboard 'shagging Giggsy'. Hello P45 in real life.

He rubbishes one of his colleagues in front of his class and hands pupils' books round in the pub, whereupon his colleagues make up marks for them. If he is supposed to be on the same wavelength as his class, why does he not give them the respect of actually reading what they have written?

Can you imagine a series called *Doctors* in which the central character engages in sexual teasing with a patient, criticises another doctor in the partnership in the waiting room, and then doles out prescriptions at random? *Carry On* film yes, documentary-type drama no.

The truth of the matter is that most jobs are full of undramatic routine, of little interest to the public, so televised versions have to spice up the action. If this Simon character were a real teacher, then his constant prowling round the room would give his pupils a stiff neck and he would be carried out by the end of the day. But the storyline has to suggest he is urgent, vibrant, in touch with adolescents.

The result of this need for drama is that most series about people's jobs are largely false: police officers solve intricate murders every week, doctors and teachers romance one another, perform professional miracles. As Michael Parkinson once said, the popular Saturday night BBC programme *Match of the Day* is not edited highlights, it is all the highlights. The resulting 10 minutes of end-to-end action may bear little resemblance to the other 80 minutes of routine passing and tackling.

Consequently no drama series about teaching gets it right. How about this? Episode 1, Simon fills in the register, but then loses his pen; Episode 2, Simon explains the past participle to year 9 one wet Friday afternoon; Episode 3, Simon actually marks a set of books himself, while drinking a nice cup of Horlicks; Episode 4, Simon doesn't get through the pay threshold, so he writes a polite letter of complaint to the DfEE. I can't see it knocking up too many peak-hour viewers on a Wednesday night.

Alternatives to false realism include the *Hill Street Blues* mixture of actuality and comic caricature, the fly-on-the-wall documentary about real people instead of actors, and the outrageous slapstick of series like *Please Sir* or the *Carry On* films, which make no pretence of being anything other than farce.

Grange Hill is recognisable as an urban comprehensive, but, though well written, directed and acted, is unlike a real school. A few years ago there was a scene in which the class moved from quiet to riot inside 3 minutes. Every single pupil ended up throwing things around the room. I have seen teaching in some of the toughest cities in the world, but even in very badly behaved classes many pupils are mere spectators.

To Sir with Love was enjoyable syrup, *Blackboard Jungle* menacing but too neatly resolved for a city like New York. The ultimately convincing drama about teaching is yet to be written.

I must start work immediately on my own realistic television series. I shall call it *Scriptwriters*. It begins with Simon, a twenty-something writer who has some really wacky pals. They all go to the pub one night, get drunk and then scribble on the back of beer mats the shooting script of a film about a praying mantis which can drive a Mondeo. In the second episode it wins an Oscar. Sounds realistic to me.

6 April 2001

What we'll do on our holidays

Fed up with all those 'What to do in the Summer' features in newspapers and magazines? Do not despair. Here is one specially for teachers.

Play 'Spot the schoolie'. See if you can pick out which fellow holidaymakers are connected with schools. Tell-tale signs to look for are:

Teachers:
- have elbow patches on their wetsuits
- do crossword puzzles in red biro
- count people on and off buses, twice
- shout at children who walk too near the edge of the kerb
- organise a football match between the waiters and the porters, giving everyone a bib
- divide each hour into 15–15–20–10-minute activities (primary only).

Heads:
- pick up litter on the beach
- stop people walking on grassy banks when it's raining
- stand up in breakfast and say 'I've received a complaint from a member of the public about poor behaviour outside the hotel'
- make people in queues stand in a straight line, no pushing
- explain 'PANDAS' and 'the Autumn Package' to bewildered foreigners.

Governors:
- always carry a sheaf of A4 papers under their arm, even in dinner
- ask whether the tour bus was booked by competitive tender
- go round soliciting the opinions of parents about the holiday
- walk up and down the beach giving out newsletters on fundraising.

Food to eat abroad if you're homesick for British education:
- cock-up au vin
- tripe *à la mode de Caen*
- pig's ear
- scrambled brains

- cold turkey
- fool's pudding
- SATsumas
- hard cheese

Simple cures for teachers' holiday problems:
- constipation – tell them Ofsted are coming the second week in September
- stomach upset – look at a pile of unmarked books, acts as an emetic
- plane delayed – take sixty random numbers and calculate value added between first thirty and second thirty
- hotel poor – rate everything as 'below the national average', then put hotel under special measures and demand an action plan
- lousy waiter asks for a tip – either say 'Don't back horses', or demand written information under five headings and then write on it 'Standards not yet met, so you're not going through the pay threshold.'

Summer vacation professional development courses

Smarm Training Plc offer the following one week courses in El Dorado Hotel Benidorm (£499) or the Internazionale Skegness (£999):

1 August **Crawling to the top;** bootlicking, obsequiousness, flattery and a host of other topics covered on this useful course for career advancement.

8 August **Managing a school in the 21st century;** aimed at head teachers; topics include climbing the wall, tearing out hair, throwing a fit and buttock clenching.

15 August **Cordon bleu courses in France;** learn how to cook the books, grill inspectors, roast miscreants.

22 August **What to do if parents complain their children aren't stretched;** course covers the 'medieval technique' (using a rack) and the 'gravity method' (swinging from beam with weights attached to feet).

Finally, if you're getting bored, plan your own 'eating hour' (15 minutes hors d'oeuvres, 15 minutes main course etc.), work out how many valium tablets you can buy with your £2,000 threshold pay, or write a limerick about Ofsted (There was an inspector called Rick . . .).

27 July 2001

Projects come out of the closet

The news that primary teachers were beginning to do topic and project work once again was most welcome. Young children enjoy getting involved in something that relates to the real world around them and it was a pity that teachers were ever made to feel sordid and unpatriotic for following their professional instincts.

Provided the work is demanding and well informed, there is nothing wrong with projects. Indeed, they bear more resemblance to adult life in the twenty-first century than much else children might undertake. Unfortunately some project and topic work was shallow and rambling, getting the whole genre a bad name.

Contrary to popular belief, the 1967 Plowden report did not offer an uncritical endorsement of such frippery. It stated quite unequivocally that school subjects should not be buried under fuzzy, ill-focused activities. The best project work has always seized children's imagination, persuading them to work on their topic way beyond the constraining confines of their classroom.

Some children remember their projects for years after they have left school. My most memorable was on York Minster at the age of 10. Although we were each given our own bit each to research (I had the magnificent Five Sisters window) the whole class knew the place inside out.

When we eventually went to visit it the guide was astonished at these little junior-school plebs from 50 miles away pontificating on about architectural styles, freely using the terminology of cathedral architecture. Years later, when it was partly destroyed by fire, I could sense my former classmates weeping collectively at the desecration.

At its worst, however, project work could corrode young brains. One of the most boring projects I can ever remember was a two-term effort on the topic 'Water'. For six months children poured it, weighed it, measured it, drank it, painted with it, and no doubt passed it. They read the history and geography of it, the turning into wine of it, its chemical formula, its properties when boiled, frozen, stamped on, juggled with. In the end they were so sick of the damned substance, it was the exact opposite of being lost in a desert: they never wanted to see a canal, a lake, an ocean, or a tap again as long as they lived.

Nonetheless it was outrageous that teachers were ever harassed out of topic and project work, as if any form of it must be inherently evil. So how has it come about that many schools have restored it? Did groups of primary teachers meet in secret locations, heavily disguised as an undertakers' convention, or prance around in funny dress pretending to be Morris dancers or freemasons?

Was there a disco in an underground cavern, where project enthusiasts could meet in safety without fear of being outed by traditionalists as the sons and daughters of Satan? 'I tell 'ee, Mrs Worthington, yon lass of thine will rot in hell for that there project on Carrots Across the Curriculum.'

Poor old John Dewey was demonised by the right wing for his historic part in the popularity of project work. In his 1938 book *Education and Experience* he actually stressed that teachers may have to intrude more, not less, if children are to capitalise on their experience, but he was accused of being a permissive trendy, responsible for the undermining of orderliness and indeed of society.

Yet all he did was recognise that young children in particular can more easily make sense of the world if they study it as it is, directly, with personal involvement, not just in a bookish way. What he wrote was self-evident, rather than anarchic or anti-social. Bully for those teachers sensible enough to reintroduce project work, not as a replacement for other forms of teaching, but as a useful part of their rich armoury. I hope they are not vilified once more.

My taboos for any project fan wanting a trouble-free life are as follows. No silly topics. No long-winded projects that die after a week but then have to stagger on posthumously. No pretending that some piddling interdisciplinary enquiry has covered the universe, making further study unnecessary. No copying out wholesale from the Internet. And definitely no projects on sex education.

One of our local right wingers, when arguing for a complete ban on sex education, used to say that if children learn about something in school they will enthusiastically put it into practice. Alas, as a modern linguist I can only say how I wish that belief were true. In reality, a boring project on sex education would be the most effective form of birth control ever devised.

25 October 2002

Watch with Big Brother

When I read that the Department of Education and Skills was going to spend 10 million a year setting up a teachers' television channel it was hard to know whether to laugh or cry. A channel dedicated to education might be handy, if it offers interesting programmes about teaching and learning, but it could be an unmitigated disaster.

There is some stunning visual material for education and, if the channel captured the best programmes, it could offer a very valuable service to schools. The question really is, however, whether this sort of teaching aid is better provided through such media as the DVD ROM nowadays, rather than a conventional TV channel.

A brilliant BBC science programme about floating and sinking, which I have sometimes used, showed a camera on board a lifeboat as it rotated 360 degrees. It offered a crisp, beautifully illustrated explanation in just a few seconds. This is the kind of phenomenon that film can portray superbly. It is very hard for any teacher to match top-quality television with normal cheap classroom resources.

I hope the DfES will resist the temptation to have any kind of input to the actual programmes, despite providing the capital for them. With the best will in the world an 'official' channel would be a total turn-off.

At its very worst just imagine a channel that bombarded teachers twenty-four hours a day with propaganda about government initiatives, schemes of work and messages about the latest official targets. There could be giant screens in every playground with teachers chanting in unison 'We will meet our targets'.

That nightmare scenario would be like George Orwell's *1984* and the Ministry of Truth. The consolation is that rebels could chant 'Hate, hate, hate!' and throw out-of-date textbooks at the screen.

Fortunately I have managed to get hold of the schedules for this new teachers' channel, so here is an exclusive preview of a typical day's programmes.

Teachers' Channel Programme Schedule

1:00 One Foot in the Grave   Richard Wilson visits another school staffroom.

1:30 Robot Wars   The DfES Standards and Effectiveness Unit takes on the Number 10 Policy Unit.

2:00 Only Fools and Horses   A recruiting film for the teaching profession.

2:15 Star Trek   Government policy makers beam down from *Starship Enterprise* with new initiatives from the planet Zarg.

3:30 University Challenge   Teams of academics compete to see who can charge the highest top-up fees.

4:00 Wish You Were Here . . .?   An early retired teacher sits on a Greek island and waves two fingers at the camera.

4:30 Full Circle with Michael Palin   Old ideas that have resurfaced. The intrepid explorer shows how 1970s Educational Priority Areas became 1990s Education Action Zones and then disappeared again.

5:30 Antiques Roadshow   Michael Aspel and the experts put a value on some of the more elderly lay inspectors.

6:15 Stars in their Eyes: Education Special   A firm of educational consultants sings 'I Left my Brain in San Francisco' and Chris Woodhead does his impression of Sid Vicious.

7:00 You've Been Framed   Hilarious videos of the chemistry teacher who accidentally set fire to an inspector's trousers and the deputy head who woke up from a dream and found she really was taking assembly wearing only a very short vest.

7:35 The National Lottery: Jet Set   Eamonn Holmes poses questions to six unpopular head teachers and the last survivor is sent on a week's holiday to Albania, while the Thunderball draw offers the chance for one lucky school to win an exercise book.

8:10 Casualty   The paramedics are called out to a school that has just failed its Ofsted inspection.

9:00 SAS Jungle: Are You Tough Enough?   Sgt Eddie Stone sends the remaining three survivors from the Borneo jungle to teach a Year 9 class.

10:00 Murder in Mind   A studio full of head teachers confronting junior minister Stephen Twigg about his letter urging them to meet their targets.

11:00 Lethal Weapon   Mel Gibson ticks thousands of boxes for a class of thirty 5-year-olds.

12:00 Closedown   Another inner-city school is put into special measures.

14 March 2003

All is mad in leadership and war

From time to time the government manages to trump even its own aces in the lunacy game. Forget the two committees they set up to look into the problems of duplication, we are talking serious derangement here.

I refer, of course, to the Leadership Incentive Grant, or LIG, a scheme for giving head teachers several hundred thousand pounds, in some cases to sack themselves and their senior colleagues.

A Leadership Incentive Grant is designed, in theory, to improve management in schools, but according to ministers it can be used to 'take out' heads and senior teachers who are not thought to be doing their job properly. The language of warfare and the SAS may be contemporary, but it is not the most thoughtful use of terminology. In the words of a phonics reading scheme: the LIG is big, it will tig the prig who does not give a fig.

Imagine the conversation.

'Here's three hundred-plus grand for you.'
'Oh, that's very kind. What's it for?'
'To buy a big gun for you to shoot yourself and your colleagues
    with, you clueless bastards.'

In the circumstances it might be better to call the scheme Utterly Nutterly, or, if the departing head is allowed to keep all the loot, a SPRIG (Spend Posterity Rolling In Gold).

Take it from me, if this goes ahead as planned there will be mayhem. Of course every effort must be made to improve management in schools amongst heads, deputies, heads of department and senior teachers, but macho talk about 'taking people out' demeans the whole operation.

WE'RE TALKING SERIOUS DERANGEMENT

Furthermore there will be endless wrangles about who is incompetent and who is merely working against the odds.

This plan has the dabs of the Number 10 policy unit all over it: the tough-guy talk, the detachment from reality, the central control over schools' plans. Why use finesse when a sledgehammer is available? I suspect this war against heads and teachers will lead to a fair bit of collateral damage.

However, I do not want to be entirely negative about the matter, so perhaps I can help by setting up a Seniors Assassination Squad. We in the SAS will do the necessary 'taking out' of heads thought to be useless as cheaply and expeditiously as possible, using all the latest technology for this sort of operation, so there will be no need to prove anyone is not up to the job, nor hold lengthy tribunals. Here is a short description of some of our weaponry.

Using drones

This involves hiring several really incompetent teachers who never lift a finger. Eventually the head and senior staff all resign in despair, saving thousands in compensation and payoffs.

Cluster bombs

Put the school into a cluster of other schools that are staffed by heads who are completely mad. After a while targeted heads believe they are also crazy, known in the psychiatry textbooks as *folie à deux*, and retire to the rest home for the terminally knackered.

Bunker busters

We bombard heads with so many official letters and initiatives they become beleaguered and withdraw to their study. When the postie calls one day with an even more massive bag they meekly come out with their hands up and retire voluntarily. Or has that one been done already?

Laser-guided target missiles

One of our SAS team shines a laser beam on to the school. Just when the school has met its existing targets another more demanding set (including, where necessary, the call for 110 per cent of pupils to reach the required standard) is fired along the beam with deadly accuracy, landing inch perfect on the head's desk without even breaking a window. The poor beggar quits in despair.

Snatch squads

If all else fails a group of us in full combat gear will rush the stage during assembly, grab any senior staff thought to be falling short in their performance and carry them bodily out of the hall. No questions asked, no hearings, no evidence. A clean snatch.

Once we have cleaned up educational leadership, we in the SAS will turn our hands to other fields of endeavour, where the same sort of jocular perversity is needed. Alongside the LIG there will be a BIG (Bankrupts' Insolvency Grant) so that businesses can be paid to give away their products to customers instead of charging for them. Our Politicians' Ignorance Grant, PIG, will be available for politicians who want to campaign for their opponents in the next election.

There will also be a CIG (Complete Idiot Grant) to 'take out' the goon who dreamt up the whole barmy idea of paying people to sack themselves. Spike Milligan must be turning in his grave.

25 April 2003

six

Keep taking the prescription: commandments from on high

One powerful form of control mechanism is the legal power to prescribe. Telling teachers exactly what to do makes them dependent. Politicians and their agencies began to decide how many minutes must be spent on each section of a primary teacher's lesson.

Every literacy hour in the primary school had to have four parts, the first two lasting 15 minutes each and consisting of whole-class teaching. The next involved 20 minutes of individual or group work, with not more than two ability groups, while the final segment was 10 minutes of whole-class revision. Yet every maths lesson only had to have three parts. Rub your eyes in disbelief if you were on Pluto when it happened.

Those training as teachers in primary and middle schools had to pass 851 prescribed competencies: 851 ticked boxes to become a teacher. It was the 1 that irritated me — utterly obsessive. Government enforcers, Ofsted and the Teacher Training Agency acted like an invading army. No wonder military metaphors were rife in education.

When the prescriptions were clearly failing the pressure became even more intense. Under this macho style there was no prospect of dead horses being buried, they had to be flogged onwards. Head teachers were awarded larger salaries, but their souls were not for sale, so most accepted their bounties gleefully and carried on obeying common sense.

Teachers were offered performance-related pay. The first £2,000 bonus was gained by almost everyone, but it made little impact on people's hostility to the way they were treated. Many objected to their creativity being squeezed out by official prescriptions. Instead of learning to write with verve and imagination, children studied the aerodynamics of phonemes, morphemes and digraphs, and even revivals of old favourites like *Janet and John* did nothing to dilute the tyranny.

On the warpath with Spiffy

Why does education use so many military metaphors? It must be nostalgia for the 1940s. You would think that World War 3 had broken out to read some newspaper stories about education. Schools are 'beleaguered'. Superheads are 'parachuted in' to rescue failure. Teachers are the 'troops', heads 'run a tight ship'. It is complete tosh.

Any normal professional debate about a commonplace educational issue soon becomes a 'battleground' with two opposing factions 'lined up' against each other, before someone 'fires the first round'. Everyone tries to 'capture the middle ground', while 'taking no prisoners' of course, until one side emerges 'victorious' and goes on to 'claim the spoils'. Bang bang, I'm king of the castle.

How on earth, for example, does 'parachuting in' actually work? I suspect that, in reality, someone merely says, 'Let's get old George in, he'll soon sort them out', whereupon old George downs his gin and tonic, removes his cardigan, puts on his least threadbare St Michael suit and swans off to ratchet Gasworks Comprehensive up the league tables.

To read the military account of events, however, you would think there was some secret airbase where superheads are trained in readiness for action. Probably in a camouflaged hangar in deepest Norfolk, at this very moment the crack Superhead Squadron is gearing up for action after their basic training, just as in those 1950s war films with Richard Attenborough and Kenneth More.

So let's go the whole hog, mix up the metaphors, clear the decks, splice the mainbrace, chocks away, look for the hun in the sun, prang the beggars, give Jerry a thrashing, back to blighty, damned good show all round, angels one five, fancy a snifter, mine's a double, tickety boo old bean, roger and out. Norfolk, here we come.

> 'Right chaps, pay attention. This is it. We're going in.'
> 'Sir, have we got time to ring our loved ones?'
> 'Sorry Spiffy. Hun's on the warpath, I'm afraid. Time to scramble. Now some of us may not come back, so let's just pause to think briefly of the folks back home, and then it's time to get airborne.'
> 'What about kit, sir?'

'It's standard issue on this mission. Make sure you've got your two key documents: Charles Atlas's *You Too Can Have a Body Like Mine* and your *Bluffer's Guide to the National Curriculum*. Then you should have your list of sound bites.'

'The sound bites are a bit dicky, sir. Any chance of some new ones?'

'No can do, Fortescue, you'll have to make do with the old ones. Stick to your top three sound bites, if possible, that's: "Tough targets will be set", "Firm action will be taken" and "No stone will be left unturned in our quest for higher standards and expectations". Keep using the word "tough" in every sentence.'

'What do the sound bites mean, sir?'

'Mean, Simkins? We're about to parachute in and you talk about meaning? Damn it, man, we're here to rescue failing schools, not ponce about doing a bally philosophy degree. Now if you look at the map, you'll see where we're going. Jenkins, you and Taffy take out Swinesville School and Community College.'

'Is that both of them, sir, or just the one?'

'Both. The Community College bit is just a temporary hut with a half-sized snooker table and a juke box. If your chute doesn't open and one of you roman candles straight into the bike shed, the other one scrapes him off and buries him under a bush. Kipper, you take command of Scumbag Primary. Have you got your spelling tests?'

'Roger, sir.'

'Once you land, chute packed tight and hidden behind the dustbins. Hush Puppies on and straight into the staffroom. As soon as you open the door, lob number one sound bite "Tough action will be taken" and then suspend the first three pupils you meet in the corridor, for dumb insolence. Any questions before we scramble?'

'Just one, sir. If I don't come back, could you . . . I mean, supposing by tomorrow I've, well, bought it, would you mind awfully taking this parcel round to Felicity? It's got great senti-mental value.'

'Of course, Spiffy. What is it?'

'It's my £70,000 a year salary cheque.'

19 February 1999

Making a meal out of lessons

A group of heads trolled along to a training session on how to identify good teachers. Enter, stage right, chap with armful of overhead projector transparencies, stopwatch, written schedule: 3 minutes to talk about slide 4a, 90 seconds for slide 12b.

'Flustered' was the word used afterwards to describe his performance. It seemed the ultimate irony that the person purporting to be an expert on the identification of effective teaching was himself a poor exponent of it.

Even worse was the reason for his downfall: practising the current belief that teaching is merely a formula, reducible to a dreary sequence of pre-timed globs, detached from any context, unresponsive to audience (unless it says so in the handbook).

It reminded me of the errors made by some trainee teachers who, through lack of experience and confidence, feel obliged to stick like superglue to their lesson plan, irrespective of how it is progressing.

'What do you do if children throw paper aeroplanes at you?' I was

STICK TO THE PLAN LIKE SUPERGLUE

once asked by a student teacher with discipline problems. It was like a head teacher wondering what to do if 400 pupils storm the platform during assembly. 'Run like hell' is the answer, but once in a safe sanctuary, work out why it happened.

In this case the hapless student had pre-planned 20 minutes during which to introduce her worksheet. In reality 5 minutes would have been plenty, but she was so worried about running out of material before the end of the lesson that she flogged on, against the evidence of her own eyes, as bored pupils turned worksheets into flight craft and floated them around the room.

Effective teaching is dynamic and responsive, not static and over-programmed. Should every lesson end with 15 minutes of review, as some advocates of the robotic approach suggest? It would be death by a thousand revisions.

A heavy session on Boyle's Law might well merit this amount of review, but different topics could require regular shorter revisions along the way. I often end lessons with one or more questions: 'Do you know why . . . ? You don't? We'll find out tomorrow.' This and other approaches are not always in the androids' handbook.

There is an argument, of course, that atomising something too finely, like our friend with his armful of transparencies did, is not only an unsuccessful strategy, but may even confuse people about what they already know. Some subjects are best learned in discrete bits, others need a more global approach.

Here is my pre-programmed course on how to make something familiar, in this case eating a meal, a touch more formidable by dismembering it. I shall leave out numerous steps for simplicity.

Preliminary set-up (15 seconds):
(1) Approach table, (2) pull back chair approximately 1 m, (3) move to front of chair, (4) lower bum until resistance encountered, (5) shuffle forward to comfortable position (see separate handbook for definition of 'comfort' and on approved method of performing this operation), (6) thank meal server for presentation of food, or serve self using implements provided and following methods in handbook.

Consolidation and empowerment (30 seconds):
(6) Take fork handle (not pronged end) in left hand, (7) grasp knife handle (not blade) in right hand, using Thoroughgood's index finger grip (Steinberg's penholder variant not permitted), (8) visually select first piece of food to be tasted, (9) insert fork to a depth of up to 1 cm, (10) draw knife backwards and forwards across food four times, (11) sever bite-sized piece.

Consumption (10 minutes):
(12) Using fork only, transfer severed food from plate surface to mouth (orifice immediately below nose), (13) open mouth and insert food, (14) close mouth and bring upper and lower jaw together thirty times (meat), ten times (mashed potato), zero times (school lunch, just close eyes and swallow whole, inserting two Rennies immediately), (15) repeat process until plate clear, (16) on conclusion slide either side of knife across tongue (working-class diners only), or emit noisy explosion of wind from mouth, saying 'By gum, that were a decent bit o' snap' (Yorkshiremen only).

A full set of OHP transparencies is available. I hope you enjoy your pre-programmed cock-up au vin.

12 May 2000

Dear Mr Head, give us £2,000

Dear Elspeth

You asked me for a response to your threshold application, which I have now received. I cannot, of course, give you any official feedback until after the external assessor has been. As head teacher I have to act correctly throughout.

You have followed the proper format, but I must point out that applications have to be submitted on the official form, so your two pages of lined Oxford pad, followed by three sheets of lilac scented note paper, may be deemed unacceptable.

I am also wondering whether your somewhat flippant prose style may count against you in the eyes of the external assessor. For example, in your cover note you talk about 'giving it a whirl' and state that your application is submitted 'with the same pathetic optimism as my weekly purchase of a ticket for the national lottery'.

In the career details section you then write the single word 'dogsbody' as your current post and describe your specialism as 'preaching to the unconvertible'. I don't personally mind your little joke putting my Christian name down as 'Genghis', but again I wonder how the assessor will react.

The evidence offered under the heading 'knowledge and under-standing' is a little sparse. While the notes of guidance mention preparation for the new national curriculum, I am not sure of the wisdom of devoting this section entirely to a description of how you and your class have pulped shelves full of old national curriculum pamphlets and recycled them as papier mâché nodding poodles.

The 'teaching and assessment' section really invites you to describe your teaching strategies. Although the notes of guidance cite how teachers deal with bullying as a possible area for comment, this was meant to refer to bullying amongst pupils, not to your view of the role of the deputy head in this school.

However, it is in the section where you have to describe pupil progress that you are in most difficulty. Your opening remark surely overstates the situation: 'The average IQ in my class resembles that of a swarm of gnats, so it would need a literacy and numeracy decade every day to make any progress, let alone a mere hour.'

Incidentally, the phrase 'P-levels' in the guidance notes refers to performance levels in special schools, not to how high the boys in your class can 'piddle up the toilet walls', as you put it. Your claim that this is 'much higher than it was last September' will not, I am afraid, qualify as value added evidence.

I have to say that I was rather hurt by your response to section 4 of your application, on wider professional effectiveness. To describe our School Development Plan as 'the greatest piece of fiction since *War and Peace*' is a gross insult to the deputy head and myself, who spent many hours writing it. Your dismissal of our whole-school INSET days as being 'about as stimulating as toothache' was also rather unkind.

Unfortunately the final section on professional characteristics does not add to your case. There is space here to describe what you do towards team building with your colleagues in the school. To write cynically, as you did, 'There is nothing we wouldn't do for each other, so I do nothing for them and they do nothing for me', is a missed opportunity.

You ask, in your note to me, whether there is anything I can do to influence the external assessor, 'like slipping something into his cocoa'. The assessor will, of course, work entirely independently and I hope you were only joking when you threatened to dress up in Dracula make-up during his visit.

Our external assessor is indeed the same person who used to be head of Lower Swineshire Primary School, but although there were some criticisms of his school in their Ofsted report, it is not true to say that it was the worst report since Dotheboys Hall, nor is it fair to refer to his £350 a day assessor fee as 'blood money'.

It is kind of you to offer to pay for me to accompany you to Benidorm if you are successful, but I shall be holidaying in Skegness.

9 June 2000

Tips on flogging dead horses

There is nothing worse than an idea or an initiative which has had its day. Once the wretched thing has expired, no amount of chivvying or public relations guff will breathe life into it. Like the *Monty Python* parrot it is dead, deceased, a stiff.

The macho style of human management is just one such dead horse. It never really caught on at grass-roots level in education, because most heads and other people in senior positions were far too smart to practise a style of control that was demeaning to professional people. Only the odd pompous prat could be seen strutting around, laying down the law, muttering vacuously about people needing 'the smack of firm management'.

The difficulty was that macho management became expected in the 1990s. It was assumed to be the norm, despite the embarrassing fact that it rarely worked. The central conviction was that Genghis knows best.

As a result initiatives in education started to come from above. The government dreamed them up, firm management was then expected to 'deliver' them. Any head who appeared unwilling to order teachers around was a ninny.

This reliance on naked power has produced the greatest crisis in education for decades. Ask most teachers, especially those who come in from industry as mature entrants, why **GENGHIS KNOWS** they originally wanted to teach and before **BEST** long they will use words like 'imagination', 'initiative', 'responsibility'. People want the challenge, so no-one talks the language of robots: 'dependence', 'blind obedience', 'servility'.

It was the nation's good fortune that two-thirds of teachers were over 40 during the 1990s, so most managed to make even the most monumentally stupid initiatives work by using their professional experience to adapt them.

By the year 2006, however, half of teachers will be over 50. We will only recruit sufficient high-quality replacements if the job is clearly seen to be one for those with imagination and initiative, and with their genitals intact. 'Wanted: 200,000 castrati' is not likely to be a successful advertising slogan.

Macho management may be a failed idea, but it is devilishly difficult to see it off. Accompanying structures and processes, like the crass style of school inspection and league tables, are firmly in place, difficult to dismantle without appearing to be a weed in the eyes of the public. All the dead horses are lying there, just waiting to be flogged.

I have been looking at a set of strategies for rescuing the irredeemable which were originally compiled for American business. Here is my adaptation for education: twenty desperate ways forward, whenever flogging a dead horse appears not to be succeeding.

1. Set up a committee to revive the horse.
2. Put on an INSET day to improve teachers' riding ability.
3. Buy a bigger whip.
4. Sack the rider and hire a new one at a larger salary.
5. Say things like 'Funny, it's never done that before'.
6. Get the children to write a poem about it.
7. Send it to a hotel for five days to train as an inspector.
8. Make reviving it a central part of the school's citizenship plan.
9. See if it can pass the threshold assessment; everyone else did.
10. Arrange a visit to another school to see how they ride dead horses.
11. Ask it to chair the Education Committee.
12. Insist that the horse is not actually dead, just in need of performance management.
13. Pay a large fee to a private company to ride the dead horse.
14. Harness several dead horses together, see if that increases speed.
15. Establish a working party to draw up a list of uses for dead horses.
16. Squeeze it into the curriculum under 'Life and Living Processes' (dead version).
17. Rewrite the horse's job description, deleting any reference to 'breathing'.
18. Get Ofsted to label it as a 'failing horse', then apply to become a Horse Reviving Action Zone with a special government grant.
19. Train it as a maths teacher; everyone has to be willing to teach maths nowadays.
20. If all else fails, try the usual solution: promote the dead horse to a senior position.

3 November 2000

Leave Bill and Ben to rot in peace

The whole nation is awash with comebacks – Janet and John, Bill and Ben the flowerpot men – all reincarnated in a new politically correct form. So what have they been doing for the past few years? Were they living on social security, sulking or just biding their time till the nation called?

I can now reveal exclusively that Bill and Ben spent the late 1980s designing the national curriculum and writing assessment documents, before moving on to national vocational qualifications in the 1990s. 'The flobbalobba range statements and the lobbalibby little weeeeeed performance indicators . . .' It is obvious in retrospect, but we never spotted it at the time. Janet and John became teachers.

> 'Look Janet, look. I'm having a nervous breakdown. I'm climbing a tree instead of taking Year 9.'
> 'Can I have a nervous breakdown, John, just like you?'
> 'No Janet, no. I like helping daddy in the garden instead of filling in forms.'
> 'I'm a primary head teacher, John. I like staying at home and helping mummy iron the clothes, because Ofsted are in school this week.'

It is all very well bringing back characters from the past, but for me they are rooted firmly in their time and should be left there.

Would Robin Hood look right wearing combat gear with a Kalashnikov in his hand? Suppose Julius Caesar made a return visit to Britain, and announced, 'I came, I saw, I set up a quango'?

What if Dick Whittington arrived in London, only to hear the bells saying, 'Turn again Whittington, thrice redundant from dot.com firms' and ended up selling the *Big Issue*? Or if Little Red Riding Hood visited her granny and found her cottage had been bulldozed, swallowed up to make way for a multiplex cinema?

These children's figures from the past should have protection orders slapped on them. I do not want to open a revamped reader from my childhood and discover that Old Lob is now running in the 2:30 at Sandown, six to four favourite for the Wheatibangs Handicap. Nor should he be sent to the knacker's yard. Just let the poor beggar carry on munching grass like he always did, dignity intact, locked in his time warp.

All kinds of horror could ensue. The elves will refuse to work nights. The shoemaker will in any case be bankrupt, because anyone who sells shoes for the price of the leather deserves to go bust. It's a dog eat dog market out there. No rescue for lame ducks, or innumerate shoemakers.

The line must be drawn, or there will be no end to the sacrilege committed under this desperate drive to modernise. Before you know it Snow White and the seven dwarfs will be demanding a minimum wage, the Wicked Queen will have been sent on a personal relationships awareness course, and Dopey will be a lay inspector.

Who will be the next revered figure to be dragged into the twenty-first century? Could it be Andy Pandy and his friend Teddy?

Andy and Teddy always had a race. Irrespective of who won, they would stage a second race in which the other would triumph. The score was perpetually one all. Will Teddy now be whitewashed five nil, like some hapless England international team, just to prepare children for the cruel reality of adult life?

I see nothing but botched disasters ahead. In a refurbished French reader the Laval family will go on a package holiday to Benidorm instead of crossing the Alps. A new version of my childhood maths book will ask, 'If one fast food operative can make fifty triple super whopperburgers plus fries in 13 minutes, how long will it take ten customers to throw up?'

IS NOTHING SACRED?

This updating fad will never work, so it must stop. Otherwise the results simply become more and more far fetched.

> 'Look Janet, look. I see a chief inspector.'
> 'Yes John, yes. I see him too.'
> 'What is he doing, Janet?'
> 'He is writing for a Conservative newspaper, John.'
> 'He is a Conservative peer, Janet.'
> 'I think I will do my ironing, John.'
> 'I think I will climb my tree again, Janet.'

Damn silly. Is nothing sacred?

26 January 2001

Sorry, ideas aren't appropriate

Teaching as a profession should be for people with imagination. The ability to invent and create is precious, the badge of the true professional. It must be protected like the Crown jewels. Take away imagination and we have teacher-as-machine, programmed androids, not humans with a heartbeat.

The greatest threat to teachers' invention is posed by the 'only one solution' merchants. They firmly believe that people should be told what to do every few minutes, though few go as far as Chris Woodhead did in the *Times Educational Supplement* in April 1998, when he said it was 'dangerous' for teachers to work out their own best professional practice. (I just decided, entirely off my own bat, to do some group work, and I'm still trembling with terror at such perilous folly.)

One of the favourite killer sayings of the 'only one solution' brigade is 'There is no point in reinventing the wheel'. Yes there is. If no one had reinvented the wheel we would still be rattling along on wooden ones, smashing our joints to bits. Pneumatic tyres would not exist, nor, for that matter, would hovercraft and space rockets. It is the ultimate conservative philosophy: nothing can be improved.

Millions of people are grateful that doctors use modern cures like bypass surgery, instead of sticking half a dozen bloodsuckers on your bum and saying, 'Well, there's no point in reinventing the leech, is there?' I wonder if the 'one solution' fans row across the Pacific in a boat, rather than fly (no point in reinventing the coracle), or refuse to live in a house in winter (no point in reinventing the cave).

The problem with this bloodless prescriptive philosophy is that it became intransigent orthodoxy, a means of control in the places which now have a stranglehold on education, like Ofsted, the Teacher Training Agency, the government itself.

When fashions change in a few years' time, as they surely must, no one will ever admit to having been in favour of tight prescription at the time, believe me. Everyone who espoused the 'only one solution' philosophy will suddenly suffer from amnesia, or will protest that they were the reluctant victims of some superior force.

I want to launch the Only One Solution Club. All those who believe in prescribing teachers' every move, whether it is the wretched 851 competencies for primary and middle-school trainees, or the minute-by-minute prescription of the literacy hour, can sign a charter admitting their enthusiasm. Then, a few years hence, when the whole idea is condemned as the uncreative, throttling philosophy that it is, I can get the charter out of a drawer and say, 'It was you lot, you conniving bastards.'

Should there be no signatories we must scrap detailed prescription now, today not tomorrow, before it is too late. The Key Stage 3 strategy, for example, should offer advice and guidance, a light touch, instead of suffocating creative teachers.

Imagination and professional judgement should be nurtured like a delicate orchid, not buried under tons of fertiliser. If we fail to do this, what kind of recruits, other than mindless zombies, are we going to attract to replace the 200,000 teachers leaving the profession in the coming decade?

A head teacher in a rural school told me that she wanted to take children to see lambing at a local farm and then get children to write about what they had seen. Alas, the visiting Ofsted inspector, who must have had a very narrow forehead and far too little space between the eyes, said that this was not appropriate for the literacy hour. To embrace the miracle of birth as a stimulus for writing, the weakest part of the prescribed hour, was apparently not suitable? What manifest twaddle.

So take half a stick of chalk in your right hand. Advance purposefully towards the board. Write on it 'My name is Mr Smith' (even if it is Miss Scattergood), in letters exactly five centimetres high. Tell the class to copy it on to their slates. Then say in a loud voice, 'Beep beep. I am a machine.'

No point in reinventing the Dalek, as the 'one solution' merchants like to remind us.

13 July 2001

Adjectives blight young lives

It was very sad to read of the 11-year-olds who had been so over-coached in their English lessons that many of them, apparently, produced identical words, phrases and sentences in the SATs, no matter what the topic was. Prescription has gone mad when anxiety about national test results and league-table position drives some teachers to squash children into identical cubes, as if in a 1950s steel factory.

Teaching like this is the ultimate horror: school as production line, teacher as machine, pupil as manufactured product. It is the equivalent of factory farming for children, turning out 21st-century battery hens. Learning to use our language should be alive, dynamic, imaginative, exciting, not mechanical and dreary. Chugga chugga chugga, drip drip drip.

It all reminds me of the kind of brain-deadening exercises I used to do at school. We were given a subject–verb–object sentence, like 'The boy kicked the ball'. Our task was to extend it with three adjectives or descriptors for the two nouns and three embellishments for the verb. 'How, when, where and why', the teacher used to rant. Perhaps he still wanders the streets in retirement, eyes bulging, shouting his mantra at startled citizens.

We hapless junior proles beavered away, producing such literary masterpieces as: 'On a sunny day, in Gasworks Boulevard, the tall, blond, left-handed boy kicked the round, brown, leather ball very hard', as you do when writing about the nation's favourite game. It was rubbish. The more sparky members of the class secretly penned their own versions under the desk and passed them round: 'On a sunny day the tall, brilliant, handsome boy kicked the small, weedy, boring teacher in the nuts', crude but therapeutic.

The complaint from SATs markers that children in the same class are writing in identical terms, whatever the topic, sounds bizarre. What is happening? Does it mean that, if children have had

HOW, WHEN, WHERE AND WHY some phrases about spiders drilled relentlessly into their skulls, they will use identical expressions to describe second-hand-car dealers, or mortuary attendants? 'The fat, hairy, evil-looking estate agent scuttled towards the helpless clients, spinning his lethal silky thread around their desperately writhing bodies.' Sounds apt.

Detaching language from its meaning is criminal, as well as ineffective. I once went into a school in America. 'Today's word is "radiator" ' the teacher announced. Pupils had to spell it, slice it, pickle it, put it in sandwiches, swallow it. I wondered whether tomorrow's word would be 'oligarchy' or 'photosynthesis'? 'If there's one thing I really like for my tea it's photosynthesis and chips, with plenty of oligarchy sprinkled on it.'

I used to travel to school with a friend who did A-level history. During the journey, while everyone else played hangman, he would sit clutching a much-thumbed essay, written by his own teacher when at university, desperately committing it to memory.

'The façade of Versailles had all the impish wit of Moliere, the pathos of Corneille, the melancholy of Racine, and the cow pies of Desperate Dan . . .' it read, though I may be mistaken about the last phrase. It was pure pseuds' corner prose, but it got him a university scholarship. Unfortunately, crammed to the eyeballs, he ended up with a poor degree.

Good teachers of English are perfectly capable of producing people who can write well enough to engage and excite the reader. The frightened ones, by contrast, are stuffing children's minds with identical wads of candy floss, doing nobody a service, least of all the poor beggars paralysed for life by the sheer banality of it. Worse, their classes achieve poorer grades than they would have got if writing had been made interesting.

Many newly qualified teachers say they are too terrified to try anything adventurous. They have been warned to stick like glue to QCA work schemes, no deviation, nothing so frivolous as a project. What are we doing to people? Here is the next generation, desperate to innovate, yet some are being suffocated on entry. No wonder nearly half are quitting within three years.

Let us try one more extended sentence. 'On a sunny day in Swinesville School, the incandescent, angry, browned-off teachers kicked all the mindless, mechanical prescriptions into the large, round, welcoming wastepaper basket, and then skipped off to the nearest warm, friendly, cheap and cheerful pub, where they planned some stimulating, imaginative, home-made lessons, to stop their festering, decaying, over-prescribed brains from finally turning into a fine, spongy, garden mulch.'

I hope the terror-stricken will copy it out and commit it to memory.

16 November 2001

Enough to turn us all to drink

Today's special word is 'roll'. The reason is to honour the literacy hour, before it disappears, and mark all those lessonettes that revolve around a single word. So, children, during our 15 minutes of whole-class language work we are going to use the word 'roll' as often as we can.

Education policies nowadays are not announced, they are 'rolled out'. That is, presumably, because there are so many of them they have to be kept in a large carpet warehouse on top of a steep hill. The latest policy to be rolled out is that the literacy hour and numeracy hour will be rolled up into one. Everyone will do a forward roll.

Perhaps it will be called the luminary hour. Or will there be maths and linguistics for two hours, known as the malingering hours? That should suit those teachers who are sick of being told what to do every few minutes, though it poses a dilemma for their GPs. What prescription do you give to those suffering from too much prescription?

Endless policy changes are not good for people. They are like an unending roller coaster: as soon as you have climbed up one mountain you have to whizz down the other side. A Swiss roll. Any teacher who is particularly good at such Alpine teaching will have to be called a 'roll model'.

What is worse, this switchback is founded on whimsy and political expediency, rather than on rationality, evidence or best practice. The result is a mishmash of ideas artificially squashed together. A sausage roll.

I am in favour of having a big bash on literacy and numeracy in the early years, but not of telling teachers what to do every few minutes. This demeans the profession. The structure of these hours was supposed to be based on research evidence, a huge confidence trick.

I have worked in this research field for over thirty years and there is no evidence whatsoever to support the insistence, for example, that every literacy lesson should be in four parts, or end with 10 minutes of whole-class review, irrespective of context.

It was merely a device so the government could boast that it had compelled teachers to return to traditional methods of whole-class teaching. It is a good job the same philosophy was not applied to driving instruction, making learners sit and listen to mass lectures on the aerodynamics of the clutch, instead of getting out on the road.

Immense, but hopefully not lasting, harm has been done by

pretending that there is only one way to teach and the harvest is now being reaped, as more teachers rebel against prescription, or simply quit. The more courageous simply say 'Roll off' (or words to that effect), refuse to follow the rules and use their professional judgement.

Every single bloody primary maths lesson is divided into three parts nowadays, like Caesar's Gaul. Why? Is a two-part or four-part

ROLL OVER, ROBOT

maths lesson regarded as shocking or obscene? No one forgets a good teacher, but everyone expunges an automaton from their memory banks. Roll over, robot.

If prescription is the solution then a few questions must be answered first. Why have literacy and numeracy improved faster in Wales, where they have not enforced a prescribed literacy and numeracy hour? Why have results improved more in science than in maths and English, when science has no nationally imposed strategy, nor a prescribed science hour?

If language proficiency has soared because of central prescription, as the government argues, then why have national test agencies not had to recalibrate their reading tests? The reason is simple: the average scores on them have not gone up. And why has writing been so disappointing? Because the literacy strategy neglected it, a very bad move, though sensible teachers made their own compensation.

I wonder what the new rolled-up literacy and numeracy hour will look like. As a compromise between the two perhaps there will be three and a half parts to it. Children could write a story about two minus signs who fall in love but then cancel each other out.

Key Stage 2 exams will contain questions such as: 'If you add three subordinate clauses to five conjunctions and then take away the past participle you first thought of, how many head teachers can fill a four-drawer filing cabinet with government circulars in less than an hour?'

The resultant stress of these endless rollouts is enough to make more teachers turn to drink. Roll out the barrel. The last thing we need for a vibrant future in the twentieth century is a profession pickled as herrings. Roll out the rollmops. So roll up, roll up. Let's rock and roll.

Tomorrow's special word will be 'oblivion'.

31 January 2003

A glossary for the less deceived

As the examination season gets underway one truth stands out like a shining beacon. No matter what anyone may argue to the contrary, a system in which the stakes are high will produce a similar level of anxiety to match. Teachers, parents, pupils, all feel the pressure in their daily life.

Nowhere is this better seen than in the rush to meet targets. The Internet is now awash with a huge target strategy industry. In the field of literacy alone there are schemes of work, booster classes, lists of key grammatical terms, all supposed to push up your class's literacy scores.

At school I loved grammar, having learned English, German, French and Latin for twenty lessons each week. Once at university I signed up for every philological course in sight, Old High German, Middle High German, Gothic, the lot. You want something putting into the pluperfect passive? Look no further, I'm your man.

So I am feeling rather envious of these manifold website merchants purveying their ashen-faced offerings to the grammatically challenged. It is true that words like 'homophone', 'phoneme' and 'morpheme' are more common than 'creativity', 'imagination' or 'enjoyment', but I don't want to be a spoilsport and pour scorn on them. As someone who can play the homophone by ear, I offer, albeit belatedly, my own web-type glossary, to help anxious teachers and pupils raise standards of literacy.

> **abbreviation** Something cut short, as in: 'Creativity in this school has experienced a considerable abbreviation.'
>
> **assonance** In theory the repetition of vowel sounds, e.g. 'prime time', but can also mean something donkey-like: 'Prescriptive literacy and numeracy teaching has a certain assonance about it.'
>
> **cliché** A trite or over-used phrase: 'Our standards agenda is working'; 'Teachers are as sick as a parrot.'
>
> **comprehension** 'Understanding', as in: 'The Number 10 policy unit has only a bog-standard comprehension of classroom realities.'
>
> **digraph** A psychological condition produced by the sheer predictability of the numeracy hour always having three parts to it, inducing a hatred of anything mathematical and a wish for instant death: 'At the end of every maths lesson I suffer from acute digraph.'

fiction   Anything put out by spin doctors about any educational topic.

homograph   A word which has the same spelling as another, but a different meaning: 'Ofsted tries to give a lead, but the prose in its school reports is like lead.'

homophone   A word which has the same sound as another, but a different meaning, like 'rite', 'right' and 'write': 'Margaret Hodge thinks she knows a right lot about education, but I wonder if she can actually write.'

idiomatic   A word formed from 'idiotic' and 'axiomatic', as in: 'Politicians should not tell teachers how to teach, that is idiomatic.'

metalanguage   The use of profane language, as in: 'When I asked him to take Miss Scattergood's Year 9 class he poured out such abuse I've never metalanguage like it.'

morpheme   The smallest unit that has meaning, so a word may consist of one or more of them: e.g. dog (one unit/morpheme), doghouse (two units/morphemes), DfES (several units with no meaning).

oxymoron   A foolish act by a well-educated person: 'Stephen Twigg's letter haranguing heads and teachers to meet their targets was a bit of an oxymoron.'

passive voice   The feeling of being a head or teacher nowadays in a primary or secondary school.

phoneme   A strategy for dealing with dilatory officialdom: 'If he doesn't reply to my bloody letter soon I shall just have to phoneme up.'

simile   Comparing something to something else, often using 'as' or 'like': 'When the head was given early retirement, he bought a boat and was as happy as a pig in muck.'

synonym   A word with the same meaning as another, e.g. 'policy initiative' and 'tripe', 'gobbledegook', 'belly laugh', 'utter bollocks', 'what planet are these people on?'

syntax   The duty levied by government on cigarettes and whisky.

tautology   Teaching something nobody else can understand, like 'ontology': e.g. 'I once knew a very clever bloke who tautology at the local university.'

tense   The state of most teachers by Friday afternoon.

    future tense   trainees who haven't yet started their teaching practice.

    conditional tense   people who are only willing to take on a post of responsibility if you offer them a lot of money.

    past tense   head teachers who are demob happy and don't care any more.

9 May 2003

seven

Problems, problems (aka 'challenges, challenges')

Eventually I realised what was wrong. Insiders kept telling me that Tony Zoffis was responsible for every cock-up in education. At first I thought Tony Zoffis must be an Italian bloke, but it was actually *Tony's Office*, the Prime Minister's policy unit. If you try to control everything that happens in 24,000 schools and 400,000 teachers from some remote location, there will be endless problems. Teachers are smart people, even hired by MI5 to help with security vetting, I discovered, so there is no need to rule them with an iron rod.

Remote control will in any case produce a rich tapestry of chaos. On one occasion numerous schools were sent sizeable sums of money as a reward for having improved. Unfortunately the cash went to the wrong schools, including some that had actually done badly, but all were allowed to keep it. It was pure Kafka.

Faced by so many problems a huge premium is put on staff development programmes, as if even more management training for heads and teachers will rectify the bog-ups of their masters. 'Stress management' is one of the most popular offerings, but it would surely be better not to stress people to death in the first place.

Stress and duress in turn produce their own harvest. Some people cheat. Pupils may plagiarise, while schools are tempted to exaggerate their achievements. Crawlers and quislings flourish. Politicians lie, claiming that failures are successes, or that students should pay large tuition fees for their university courses because of untold, and largely fictitious, graduate income fortunes ahead of them. Tough luck if you want to be a vicar.

Worst of all is the language of what Churchill called 'terminological inexactitudes'. By a nifty piece of linguistic deftness, the bad becomes the good, so 'cuts' become 'efficiency gains'. In this skilfully sanitised world 'problems' themselves disappear completely. They transmute neatly and instantaneously into 'challenges'.

Take Tony Zoffis' bullets away

Apparently the armed services are so short of money they cannot afford to pay for ammunition, so somebody has to shout 'bang!' instead.

'What do you do in the army then?'
'Er, I'm the bloke who shouts "bang!"'

I have been baffled for some time about a man whose job it is to shout 'bang!' at those working in education. I kept hearing his name – Tony Zoffis – over and over again.

'Where's that funny idea come from?'
'Tony Zoffis.'

According to journalists this Tony Zoffis firmly believes that attacking teachers pushes you up the opinion polls, sad if true. But what was the origin of the name Zoffis? Italian, maybe?

Then it dawned on me. There should be a glottal stop, if you'll pardon the expression, after the 'z' sound – Tonyz (glottal stop) Offis. At last it made sense. It was *Tony's Office*, the Prime Minister's hidden coterie.

The latest 'bang!' from Signor Zoffis to strafe the teaching profession, billed in the press as an 'attack', was Tony Blair's speech about comprehensive schools having too much mixed-ability teaching and not coping with able pupils. It seemed contrary to such facts as exist.

Point 1: The attack is odd, coming immediately after the record numbers of GCSE and A-level successes, including those obtaining top A grades.

Point 2: Some comprehensive schools may be poor, but as a genre they have been a success. One in ten pupils went to university in the 1960s, when they were introduced, and about 80 per cent of school leavers had absolutely nothing to show for their secondary schooling. Now only 7 per cent of pupils leave with no certificate, nearly half the population gets five high-grade GCSEs, a third go to university.

Point 3: A survey of 1,560 comprehensive schools showed mixed-ability teaching operates mainly in the first year. In the second year 83 per cent of schools use ability setting, and by the third year over 93 per cent do so (Caroline Benn and Clyde Chitty, *Thirty Years On*, David Fulton Publishers, 1996).

Another oddity was the criticism of what the prime minister called the comprehensive schools' 'one-size-fits-all mentality'. This seemed both unfair and inconsistent. Diversity is important, I agree, so why does the government lay down the same national curriculum for all schools?

Why do we have the highly prescriptive 'one-size-fits-all' literacy hour, where the government has spelled out an identical 15–15–20–10-minute pattern for every primary class, young or old, every single day?

Let us be clear what I am saying. I agree with specialist schools, education action zones, much of what the government is doing. I have seen some superb examples. I welcome the emphasis on helping all children and not just a few, and the significant sums of money for books, equipment, school buildings. I like the literacy and numeracy initiatives, but not the detailed prescription.

Nor is there anything wrong with the Prime Minister asking for a review of comprehensive schools, or of being critical when necessary. He seems a decent family man, genuinely interested in education.

I just don't think the Tony Zoffis approach to schools and teachers is right, with its language of 'zero tolerance' (fine for criminals, not for professionals), 'tough' this and 'tough' that.

One Thursday, last October, the new college for head teachers was opened. It was an excellent move, but on the previous Sunday a story was planted in a national newspaper saying that the Prime Minister would be putting the boot into teachers at the opening.

Why does Tony Zoffis spin against teachers in this way? It might win a few votes, but it is cheapskate, no way to enthuse teachers, a bit like saying, 'Join our crusade, you clueless bastards.'

I have agonised while writing this piece – walking round the room, sharpening three more pencils (funny this, I use a word processor) – since I would be mortified if Hague and his loony right-wing pals got back. But teachers deserve better than Tony

Zoffis firing verbal bullets at them and it would be dishonest not to say so.

Bang! Put him in a cupboard for a few months. He won't be missed.

22 September 2000

I spy a nation run by teachers

The news that MI5 was hiring teachers to vet its recruits was immensely cheering. It showed that the teaching profession, often vilified, had all the qualities needed to serve the nation. There have been some rum characters in the security forces of late, so who better than seasoned schoolies to flush them out?

Teachers clearly have experience that will benefit national security, but there is no limit to the other jobs they might do. Biology teachers can shorten waiting lists in the national health service: treat the odd ingrown toenail, perform an occasional transplant.

Nursery and infant teachers could take over the whole waste recycling industry. Moonlighting as lorry drivers (useful extra income for those whose threshold applications do not succeed) they transport truckloads of useless junk into school. Children then glue a few rice crispies on to each item, paint it purple and label it 'Starship Enterprise'.

Doting parents have no option but to display it on their mantelpiece for three weeks, before sneaking out furtively at midnight, while their children are fast asleep, to dump it back on the tip. Next morning the lorry driving teachers arrive and cart it all into school again. Bingo! Extra pay for teachers and the nation's intractable waste problems are solved.

But what will the teachers recruited by MI5 actually do when they commence their tricky task of flushing out potential spies? I can just picture the scene.

> 'Right, settle down, there's too much noise. Quiet everybody so I can take the register. Gary Adams.'
> 'Defected, sir.'
> 'Defected, what do you mean?'
> 'Gone over to the Albanians, sir.'
> 'The Albanians? But he didn't get a note first. If I've told you once I've told you a thousand times: nobody is allowed to defect unless they've got a signed chit from me in advance, is that clear?'
> 'Sir, Darren Rowbottom's just put ink all over my homework.'
> 'Stop that, Darren.'
> 'I can't help it, sir, my pen exploded.'
> 'Sally Baker. Where's Sally Baker?'
> 'She'll be late sir.'

'Late, why?'

'She said to tell you she's failed her A-level seduction module, so she's got to do an extra glamour and allure class with Miss Dietrich in the Mata Hari wing.'

'Well nobody told me. How am I supposed to run a vetting session when nobody tells me anything?'

'Sir, Darren Rowbottom's nicked my Minox camera.'

'Darren, give Sophie her Minox back.'

'That's not fair, she nicked my poisoned umbrella tip first.'

'Give it her back now, or you're staying in at break, and Sophie, give Darren his umbrella tip back.'

'I can't sir.'

'Why not?'

'I gave it to Tom and he's pricked his finger on it, that's why he's foaming at the mouth'.

'Oh for goodness' sake, Tom, it's only a little prick. Stop making such a fuss. Just lick it until break and then I'll get you a sticking plaster. Right, I want to get on with this vetting, so stop talking. Now, everybody empty out your pockets. Darren Rowbottom, what is all this?'

'Half a million roubles, sir.'

'Half a million roubles? Where on earth did you get that from?'

'Found it, sir.'

'You found it. Do you seriously expect me to believe that?'

'Sir, he's lying. He got it off a big bloke in a black raincoat.'

'Is that true, Darren? Look at me when I'm talking to you. I said, is that true? If you own up you won't get into trouble, I promise you.'

'It's my winnings, sir, I had a bet come up at the betting shop and it's my winnings.'

'Your winnings? What, in roubles?'

'It's a Russian betting shop, sir. Honest, cross my heart.'

'Right, that's it. I'm asking the head to exclude you permanently from MI5, so let that be a lesson to everybody. Now Darren, is there anything you want to say before you leave?'

'Just let me remove my disguise first. That's better. I can now reveal that I'm really Higgins, your threshold assessor, and I'm pleased to tell you that I will be confirming your £2,000 salary bonus.'

Security vetting? It's a pushover. Adverts for teachers to act as cardiac surgeons, archbishops, and jet pilots should be submitted immediately.

6 October 2000

They think you're great, really

The news that schools had wrongly been sent money for 'improvement' was hilarious. Apparently there was a 'statistical error', so large sums were given out incorrectly to numerous schools. Fortunately they did not have to return it. They were just required to kneel and give thanks that we are bottom of international numeracy league tables.

I like to think it was not an error, but a deliberate ploy, based on the 'expectancy effect': what you get is what you expect. Two American researchers once told teachers that they had identified certain pupils who would be making an unexpected spurt. The children had been chosen at random, but the researchers claimed they improved nevertheless, simply because their teachers expected them to. Actually the research was flawed and subsequently discredited, but it made a good story.

Perhaps this latest misplaced generosity was another expectancy experiment. Write to a few randomly chosen schools: 'Dear School, you have done so well we enclose a cheque for a large sum of money to spend on anything you want: books, equipment, six packs of lager for the staff. Have a great time on us, and keep up the good work. Yours, Sid Innumerate.' As a result the staff and pupils are so chuffed at being loved, they run their socks off and really do improve what they are doing. Brilliant.

THE BENEFIT OF THE BOG-UP

Think of all the other cock-ups that might yield excellent results. Stick a pin in a list of teachers and write to them: 'Dear Teacher, we have just been looking at all our data and you have been identified as one of the finest teachers we have ever seen. Love, Ofsted.' Proud recipients would improve overnight.

I have always been a great believer in the benefit of the bog-up. Not for me the view that an error is a catastrophe. Given a little tweak, a teeny spin, even the most monumental mistakes can be turned to advantage. We need more, rather than fewer serendipitous blunders.

Back in the early 1980s there was a salary settlement for teachers, the Clegg Award. It seemed generous at the time, until it was discovered that there was a miscalculation and people had been paid too much. Did the world come to an end? No, quite the reverse. For a short time, at any rate, teachers felt their efforts were being recognised.

This bureaucratic nightmare reminds me of Kafka's novel *The Castle*, in which a land surveyor is asked to do some work at a castle, but when he arrives nobody can tell him what he has been brought in to do. He spends the whole novel trying to find out, and at one point gets a letter congratulating him on his work, even though he has done nothing.

What we now need is yet another initiative, this time based entirely on error. We can call it the Franz Kafka Lottery Initiative. Every morning randomly chosen schools will receive munificent bounties. No more long-winded bidding processes, form filling, visiting assessors, just pure chance. The possibilities are numerous and the expectancy effect will work wonders, without wasting valuable time.

'Dear Scumbag Primary, I am delighted to say that you are the deserving winner of a Kafka (Kwantity and Finest Kwality Award) for the excellent work of your staff and pupils. You may spend the enclosed cheque on anything you choose, including trips to the Mediterranean, backhanders to staff and bets on greyhounds.'

'Dear Bogstandard Comprehensive, you have just been awarded £100,000 to support your work in . . . (enter any subject, or field of endeavour, even if they don't do it, like music, Latin, economics, pole vaulting, arm wrestling). Congratulations on your excellent record and I fervently hope this cash injection will help. Yours, Franz.'

I've got a couple of other ideas, from television shows. Put ten head teachers in the Big Brother house to vote each other out, last one wins a fortune. Or let them answer questions in a semi-circle: 'Gasworks Primary, you are the weakest link, goodbye.' People often complain that funding is a bit of a lottery nowadays, so why not go the whole hog and make it an official and well organised one?

20 April 2001

Kylie is never the right answer

I am as ready to be professionally developed as the next man, but I keep receiving notices about professional development courses that leave me baffled and confused. The latest mailing was no exception. First on the list of enticing events was a one and a half day workshop entitled *Managing Time*. Part I was a three-hour session in February, part II a whole day, one month later, in March.

It seemed strange to me. If the begetters are themselves so expert at managing time, why did they require one and a half days, spread over a month, to pass their nuggets on to others? Could they not knock it off at one sitting, in an hour maximum? I am sure Delia Smith would only need a few minutes of prime-time television ('Here's a checklist I prepared earlier').

The next one was a three-hour workshop entitled *Clearing your Desk*. Given a big brush and a waste bin I could have cleared mine in 3 minutes. I cannot see the point of attending a course on it and still having to disencumber the damned thing.

Anyway, I like an untidy desk. It is in complete harmony with my untidy mind. The world in which I live is not tidy. My desktop is a painstaking work of modern art, a future Turner Prize winner, reflecting perfectly the problematic nature of both the universe and the human condition.

Top of my list of courses to attend only if submitted to rack and thumbscrews, and there is no guarantee nowadays that this might not be a possibility for the reluctant managee, was a two-day workshop on Stress Awareness and Coping with Pressure. Two whole bloody days, again a month apart. I would be a certified maniac by the end of it, salivating, gibbering incoherently, led away gently but firmly to the Kenneth Baker Rest Home for Broken Pedagogues.

I once went to a workshop on stress. Never again. Everyone was completely tranquil, until the smug prat running it refused to start the session on time because he wanted to finish his cup of tea at leisure, saying he was showing us how relaxed he was. This and a few other self-indulgent moves successfully turned an amiable audience into foaming psychopaths, sinews standing out like ropes.

That rich experience was second only to another session on 'group building skills' in which we had to complete two jumbled-up jigsaw puzzles. I was told off by the organiser for spotting that one of the puzzles had a black streak running along the edge of each of its wooden pieces, so we split into two sub-groups and completed the puzzles within a few minutes of silence.

Apparently we should have struggled for leadership and fallen out with each other. The wizard organising the course would then have patched us up and honed our group building skills. If there is a shortcut, take it, was my conclusion, bugger the fineries.

IF THERE'S A SHORTCUT, TAKE IT

In one university department that had not done well in its external assessment they all got together and played those ice-breaking games so beloved at the beginning of management courses. An excellent paper written by one member on what needed to be done was left undiscussed, while people who had worked together for years rushed round with labels on their backs guessing who was Michael Jackson and who Kylie Minogue. It was a rum solution to their ills, creating tension rather than relieving it.

I did once go to a course on time management. The only thing I remember now is the suggestion that you should have two in-trays, one for urgent and one for non-urgent business. I still use this system. The 'urgent' tray works brilliantly, as it is empty. Unfortunately the 'non-urgent' tray is two feet high. So I talk to myself about it.

'You could throw that report away now.'
'Yes, but I might need it one day.'
'Well file it then.'
'Under what?'
'How about "QCA"?'
'That's already got fifteen fat folders and three bookshelves.'

We all end up with a unique time-management system to suit our personality and the context in which we operate. Like everyone else on the planet I am adept at deferring the things I don't want to do. Don't want to write something? Sharpen three more pencils. Odd that, since I use a word processor.

Clever people make procrastination respectable by calling it 'prioritisation'. I simply work long hours and get there in the end, grossly inefficient I know. If only I were smarter about it I would be able to clear at least a day and a half during February and March. Then I could go on that time management course.

25 January 2002

It's flying time for crawlers

It is becoming increasingly difficult to sort the real from the bogus in education. Whether one looks at people, achievement, history even, the public relations industry is hard at work. One of the reasons I like doing research is that at least it is an attempt to find out what is really happening, though researchers themselves are only human and can still give a distorted version of events.

Politicians often blacken the past so they can glorify the present and future: once we were the dunces of Europe, now we are the intellectual giants of the solar system, or will soon be if you just give us one more term in government. It is understandable because schools do the same. Is there a mission statement anywhere in the land that states, 'Some people here have just lost it, as we slide irrev-ocably down the slope of indifference'? Of course not. In public statements people present themselves in their best light and truth may be gently massaged.

It is becoming very difficult to tell, for example, whether standards for all pupils are going up when teachers are pressed, reluctantly, into strategies for beefing up league-table positions, like concentrating on pupils at the borderlines. Examination boards themselves, fearful of their competitive position in the examinations market place, are unwilling to allow the re-marking of papers by bona fide external researchers to see if standards are slipping. In these circumstances, where much is at stake, so image is vital, the annual wrangle about whether rising success rates are the result of greater efforts by candi-dates and their teachers, or grade inflation, becomes insoluble.

A high-stakes system, where schools are likely to be vilified, often unfairly, nurtures pretence and even dissimulation. Any honest confession of facing a difficulty is seen as an incurable weakness, so only the courageous dare to admit that all may not be well. Yet in a healthy society this is precisely what ought to happen. Problems should be in the open, so everyone can rally round and support.

Pupils too are under pressure, so it becomes more difficult to trace coursework plagiarism, when the Internet freely advertises assignment-writing services. I once read an essay entered for a competition by a 10-year-old. It began and ended in 10-year-old mode, but the middle was full of statements about 'householders in

England and Wales'. Some plagiarism is more subtly done and harder to detect.

Head teachers complain about inexact references when a school, anxious to be rid of someone, provides a glowing testimonial. Many years ago a college of education gave a reference for a final-year student which simply stated 'She excels at any game which does not involve the use of a ball'. Nowadays lawsuits would fly, so the tutor would be more guarded.

In these circumstances it is sometimes the smart public-relations people who make progress up the educational ladder. Fortunately the best leaders in education have got there on merit, rather than via a carefully sculptured image, skill at crawling or willingness to be a quisling, though there are some notable exceptions. I can think of one or two people, promoted beyond their modest talents, whose reference might most honestly have read 'As a crawler he leaves caterpillars standing'.

I often tell applicants for senior posts the story about the turkey and the bull. One day a bull noticed that a turkey standing under a tree was looking rather morose. 'Alas,' the turkey remarked, 'I've got wings, but I can't fly.' 'Nonsense,' replied the bull. 'It's just a matter of willpower and the right diet. All you have to do is nibble at my drop-pings, which are full of the most powerful nutrients, and then be absolutely determined.'

The turkey was sceptical, but did as she was told, nibbled at some of the bull's droppings, flapped her wings energetically and managed to lurch on to the bottom branch of the tree. 'What did I tell you,' said the bull triumphantly. 'Ah yes,' replied the turkey, 'but this is hardly flying. I'm only six feet off the ground.'

The bull exhorted her to try again and eventually, after several nibbles at cowpats and colossal flapping efforts, the turkey reached the very top of the tree. Utterly exhausted, she stood there in triumph as the bull bellowed his congratulations.

At this moment the farmer arrived, saw the turkey standing proudly at the top of the tree, picked up his shotgun and killed her stone dead.

And the moral of the story is: bullshit may get you to the top of the tree, but it won't keep you there.

5 April 2002

Earn a crust by buttering up

The news that some schools will be given extra money to dole out to teachers has certainly caused a flutter. In the United States it was common for individual performance-related pay programmes to collapse after a relatively short period and be replaced by group bonus schemes. Some of these also disintegrated eventually.

National pay scales may appear restrictive, but they do offer people a ladder of progression and a career structure. No doubt harmonious schemes will be devised for assigning the cash, but there could be mayhem if people think this latest manifestation of the market system is unfair. I can picture the scene.

'Ah, Mr Jenkins, do sit down. I'm glad you've been able to come along for a little chat. Not often we heads can do this, what with all the paperwork nowadays.'

'Thank you, headmaster, but I'm afraid I didn't understand all that jumble of letters in the note you sent me, something to do with our salaries, wasn't it?'

'Quite right, Mr Jenkins. The extra money the government has given the school for our excellent results is a bit of a headache, that's why I want to see every member of staff individually, to sort out the IBS as soon as possible.'

'IBS? I don't understand.'

'Yes, I know, new initiatives seem to come along every week in education. IBS stands for "Individual Bonus Scheme". It's another "market forces" system for rewarding hard work. The government has given the school a sum of money in recognition of our progress, so the governors and I have worked out a scheme for assigning a bonus to those who most deserve one. We rejected the FRBS solution.'

'I'm afraid I don't follow. FRBS? What does that mean?'

'Let me explain. Sorry about all the acronyms in my letter to staff, but FRBS stands for "Flat Rate Bonus Scheme", everyone would get the same amount of money. We drew up a system for calculating a separate amount, rewarding each person for individual merit. It seemed only fair.'

'I don't quite understand. I thought we were all going to get about £340, that's what it said in the papers.'

'Indeed, indeed. That is the average, but under our scheme those who really deserve it will get more.'

'Presumably that means that some people will get less.'

'Quite correct, Mr Jenkins, and that is what I want to explain. You see, we have drawn up a solution we have named OFFAL.'

'Awful?'

'No, OFFAL, it's a set of weightings, "Official Factors For Acknowledging Learning", because we wanted to put progressing up the league table at the top of our agenda. We start with £340 and then add or subtract according to the OFFAL loadings.'

'Does that mean I get more than the average because my music results have gone up this year?'

'Ah, now you've put your finger on one of the problems. Music doesn't qualify for the £100 SS premium.'

'SS, what's that?'

'It's for a "Sexy Specialism", like maths or science. Music is a NILTSU, I'm afraid.'

'NILTSU?'

'It means "Not In League Table, So Useless". In fact, teaching music was given a negative loading.'

'Negative loading? I don't understand.'

'Music, art and PE teachers have been deducted £200. The other bad news, by the way, is that you were docked a further £150 for SODOFF.'

'Pardon?'

'You're 46, you're more expensive than a newly qualified teacher, which means you had to be given a SODOFF weighting, "Salary and On-costs Dear, Over Forty Factor". That makes £350 debited altogether, so you actually owe us a tenner.'

'But that can't be right, headmaster. I work long hours, I've produced excellent concerts and carol services for years, many former pupils write and tell me they still practise music because of my teaching. What do I have to do to get more money?'

'Well, let me look at the schedule, I'd like to be helpful. Now the biggest bonus is £500 for a MOSTPNTGP, but unfortunately you don't qualify for that.'

'Why not?'

'Because MOSTPNTGP stands for "Maths Or Science Teacher Promising Not To Get Pregnant". You might still be in for a

GIEML though. That's flexible, £50 to £500, according to people's specialisms.'

'What's a GIEML?'

'It's only for people who are applying for jobs at another school: "Got Interview Elsewhere, Might Leave". Unfortunately there isn't much left in the kitty anyway, because I am pleased to say I myself have been awarded a £10,000 BUNG.

'BUNG? Does that stand for "Being Useless, Never Grafting"?'

'No, it means "Buttering Up Naive Governors".'

19 April 2002

That'll be the day that I DIY

The Design Council proposal that schools should buy their furniture from some of the more design-conscious High Street retailers, like IKEA and Habitat, is an interesting one. Those inured to working in a squalidly functional environment would welcome a bit of colour and interesting shape, other than the art teacher.

I am all in favour of anything that departs from the 'bog standard', to choose a term at random, provided that schools are not subsequently attacked for being spendthrift or trendy. There is no reason why children should not be educated in an aesthetically pleasing environment, especially when good design and low cost go hand in hand.

In Victorian and Edwardian times the three-decker school, with its electricity and running water, offered a model for pupils. Schools were a living daily reminder of aspiration. The message was clear: work hard and you too can live in modern luxury like this.

More recently, a long period of neglect in the 1980s and 1990s turned what were sometimes the same buildings into dilapidated slums, often inferior to the homes of the children educated in them. Schools became a daily reminder of desperation. The new message seemed to be equally clear: work hard, or you too could end up living in a dump like this.

If children are to receive the very best, however, will society be eager to pay, or will attractive furniture and the trappings of a decent working environment be relegated once again to the bottom of the priority list? Hankering after designer furniture may simply become yet another good intention that crumbles to dust.

If schools are to venture into the High Street it is important that what they buy is not just attractive, but also functional and reasonably priced. Over the years traditional school furnishings have not always met these three criteria.

Consider those metal tubing and canvas chairs that for years were a common institutional form of seating. They were cheap, they could be stacked high, but not for nothing were they known as 'numbums'. Sit for longer than a few minutes and the nether regions were paralysed.

Thousands of punishments were meted out to children shuffling this way and that on their wretchedly uncomfortable chairs. They were accused of fidgeting, being incapable of sitting still, but they were simply obeying a primeval drive to keep up a flow of blood to their reproductive organs, so that humanity had a future.

Teachers themselves are notorious sufferers from haemorrhoids, after years of standing for most of the day, munched sandwiches and sitting on uncomfortable wooden chairs in between times. The combination of piles and a flat wooden chair is what you would wish on your worst enemy.

If schools are to do more High Street shopping then it must all be carried out judiciously. There are many pitfalls for the unwary. Can you imagine if someone shopped at one of those places where the furniture looks very nice in the showroom, but comes in a flatpack? I still remember bitterly the wardrobe that took me a weekend and much Anglo Saxon language to assemble.

The instructions had been translated directly from the original Sanskrit and the diagrams been drawn by a cerebrally challenged Martian. By Sunday night, fingers covered in glue, mysteriously spare wooden dowels still lying in the box, I was ready to put a sledge hammer through the finished product. The thought of teachers assembling their own furniture after school from these miniature torture chambers in a box is too cruel to contemplate.

Then there were those very nice designer dining room chairs we bought that suffered from one slight drawback: the beautifully curved teak frames fractured every time someone leaned back in them. 'That was a very nice dinner, thank you.' Scrunge! Another embarrassed guest lay helpless on the floor, as we cursed the whole Danish nation for the design faults of the few.

Maybe the very idea of schools shopping on the High Street should be widened to teaching children in class. Do four sums and get another one absolutely free. Only three out of ten for your homework? Write with a brand-new Whizzo all-purpose pen and we'll double it.

This is only right, since the High Street market approach has already been applied to teachers. Meet your 2002 targets and win a new folder for your tickboxes. Brilliant at teaching maths or science? Come to our school and you'll be paid more than in some schools we could mention.

Collect our good behaviour vouchers and you can get a cash bonus. No, I tell you what. Look missus, I like your face, the wife'll kill me for this, but how about £2,000 and another grand if you meet next year's targets . . .

22 November 2002

Porkie pies given to you in 2002

Every new year starts off with great hopes that the worst of last year will be buried and everything will be fine now January has arrived. There were high and low points in 2002, but prospects for 2003 are clouded by some rather large clumps of dark satanic cumulus.

The high point for me in 2002 was all those remarkable children and teachers who raised over £200,000 for the TES campaign to provide education for their fellows in Afghanistan, after many bleak years when this fundamental human right was denied to most young people. It was a stunning example of global citizenship in action.

The low point was seeing the anguished face of a boy I had taught for GCSE in English who came into the school in August to collect his results. He had got a grade C in English, but everything else was D or E. In other circumstances it would have been a decent profile, but in our high-stakes examination system, where we rightly celebrate success, he felt a complete loser. He is a good citizen nonetheless.

Biggest laugh of 2002 was Chris Woodhead's newspaper 'advice' column. Every week questions conveniently came in about his prejudices. Mrs Nameandaddresswithheld, a regular contributor, even wrote a second letter about teacher training for her graduate daughter. Odd that mothers keep writing in about their apparently bereft, grown-up, fully graduated offspring, but the chap is lucky that the assiduous Mrs Nameandaddresswithheld shares his concerns.

Thick clouds for 2003 are gathering. The government promises to cut bureaucracy, but there is still a plan for early years teachers to have to complete a 117-item profile on 3- to 5-year-olds, with 3,510 tick-boxes for a reception class of thirty. Some idiotic local authorities have produced even bigger checklists. It is utterly disgraceful. Promises to reduce control and bureaucracy are nothing but rotten fibs.

The great argument over top-up fees for university students will resurface later this month. The debate has largely neglected one very important aspect: the devastating effect high fees would have on the recruitment of teachers.

Since I loathe the very idea of students being charged huge sums for what should be their birthright, I propose to labour the issue to death. Unless the paper on university funding addresses such matters as the future recruitment of graduates to the public services it will be a grand waste of Norwegian trees.

If top-up fees really are introduced, then 22-year-olds will emerge from university with a debt of, I suspect, somewhere between £15,000 and £70,000, depending on what they study and where. So how many of them will be prepared to work in a job where their salary will be modest, but just enough to bring them into the band where they have to pay these large sums back?

The biggest confidence trick of all was the announcement that **MORE LIES** graduates must pay for their studies because they will earn £400,000 extra as a result of getting a degree. This is complete and utter cobblers. They will do nothing of the kind. More lies.

This highly suspect figure of £400,000 was estimated on the beneficiaries of a system when only 4 or 5 per cent went to university and many of these had attended public school, were well connected or could go into family businesses. It is no basis for a situation where half the population might graduate.

Nor do I believe the promise that the poor will not pay fees. It sits alongside the proposal that students be deemed independent of their parents, which in turn means they could be charged as potential beneficiaries. Yet more porkies.

It is interesting how the views of powerful politicians affect debates on education. When I interviewed James Callaghan for Radio 4 on the anniversary of his Ruskin College speech, he told me that he had passed the eleven-plus but did not attend grammar school as his mother had no money for the bus fares. He never again wanted to see children prevented from gaining education because of the cost.

The present Prime Minister is a strong supporter of high top-up fees, but he is a wealthy and privileged man. For parents on big six-figure incomes university fees will be pocket money, but they would load a crippling burden on to ordinary folk. Were there a premium fee on science subjects, and sums as high as £15,000 a year have been suggested, it is even less likely that science graduates would enter teaching.

I wonder if Mrs Nameandaddresswithheld will write to Wooders about the matter, because he says he is in favour of top-up fees. But then, so are Kenneth Baker, Stephen Byers and, I believe, Ethelred the Unready.

3 January 2003

Wolf loves sheep's language

What's in a word? Education is full of honeyed terms nowadays, euphemisms that dress up mouldy old apple cores as luscious, freshly plucked fruit. Every new initiative is given some glorious title that makes it sound successful before it has even been launched, but merely serves to conceal the paucity of thinking beneath it, like 'advanced' schools that hadn't even started.

A few years ago the Conservative government produced a parents' pamphlet that was so riddled with errors it had to be pulped. The resultant six-figure haemorrhage was recorded as a 'constructive loss'. Try telling that to your bank manager.

Universities were promised that the present government would not cut its grant to them when tuition fees were first introduced. It was another terminological inexactitude, as Churchill used to call blatant lies, and the money has since declined by nearly 10 per cent. In our insincere world such year-on-year cuts are normally referred to as 'efficiency gains'. Chop off your leg and you learn to hop.

I have never been able to let the phrase 'deliver the curriculum' cross my lips. I will teach it, I might even 'instruct' children, but delivery is strictly for Postman Pat. Yet some people absorb fresh terms like a sponge, partly because it is thought to sound smart and up to date, and partly from the usual willingness to conform.

Take the use of the term 'K' instead of 'thousand', as in 'We need to raise 50K to become a specialist school.' I like the word 'thousand'. It is a good old Germanic term. There is nothing wrong with 'kilo' as a prefix meaning the same thing, it is just that I wonder why the would-be smart people talk of 50K.

Are they so busy that the minute fraction of breath saved will prevent them from expiring at the end of the day after their heroic efforts? Do they secretly hope that some ignorant colleague will ask 'Fifty what?' and they can feel superior explaining it? Or is it just another change of language over time, such as I normally love to see, so I should welcome it?

It is the pretentious or dishonest terms that I dislike most. Nowadays you must not 'investigate' a problem or a potential field of growth, you have to 'scope' it if you are to be in the swim and earn the respect of the peasantry. Excuse me while I just scope my toenails. No, I haven't quite got the hang of it.

Then there is the phrase 'leading edge', used to describe any idea that hides a vacuum under a web of candy floss. With some such initiatives you are left thinking, 'If that is the leading edge, what the hell must the rubbish behind it look like?'

One recently announced programme involves giving £60,000 a year (or 60K as we cognoscenti like to call it) to private schools so they too can become specialist colleges. The faint hope is that their facilities will be shared with state schools, i.e. from 2 to 3 a.m. on alternate Tuesdays. This is a magnificent example of euphemism at its best, for it is to be called the Leading Edge Programme.

It is nothing of the sort. It is a perverse and retrograde step, not a leading one. Public schools have charitable status and already get millions from the government through tax relief on donations from the wealthy. Eton is in the top 100 charities, earning some £30 million a year (known as 'a bloody enormous amount of K').

The name of the programme should be what it actually is. It should be known as the We've Got the Barefaced Cheek to Give Lots of Public Money to the Fee-paying Schools that Rich People Go To and We Hope Nobody Notices Programme.

Where will the deception of nomenclature end? The requirement that schools in poverty-stricken areas have to raise £50,000 (better known as 'far too much K') to achieve specialist status should be rebranded the Come Off It Programme.

The proposal to charge students vast top-up fees should be called the You'll All Leave University Owing 30K Project. The government should rename its Early Years Profile for children aged 3 to 5 the Believe It Or Not We're Going to Stick 117 Different Labels on Little Children's Foreheads Because We're Completely Barmy Initiative.

As Wordsworth might put it, were he around today:

> I wandered lonely as a cloud
> Through education's wondrous way,
>   When all at once I scoped a crowd
> Of programmes costing lots of K.

28 February 2003

Footnote

There are two choices when things go badly in education: laugh or cry. I prefer to laugh, because the alternative is too awful to contemplate, and anyway, why should the buggers grind you down? The low morale of many teachers has been grievous to behold, because the job they do is one of the most important on the planet. Laughter in the staffroom has kept many afloat when they might otherwise have gone under.

Professional life has become highly stressful in the twenty-first century. Everyone wants so much from the years of compulsory schooling because of the immense complexity and uncertainty of the world in which we live. I satirise politicians, but none of us can always be sure what the best course of action should be, especially when circumstances change rapidly and unpredictably.

My favourite story in recent times is one which neatly sums up all that is surreal in education: the detachment of policy from practice, the lack of understanding, the uncritical faith in private provision. It is even more appropriate because it is not even about education, though it could be.

A shepherd was tending his sheep by a country road when a brand-new Range Rover screeched to a halt next to him. The driver, dressed in a sharp Italian suit, handmade shoes, expensive sunglasses, gold wristwatch, jumped out and said, 'If I guess how many sheep you have, will you give me one of them?'

The shepherd looked at the large sprawling herd of grazing sheep and said 'Okay', so the man parked his Range Rover, connected his notebook and wireless modem, entered a NASA site, scanned the ground using satellite imagery, opened a database and 60 Excel tables filled with algorithms, printed a 150-page report on his high-tech mini printer, and said, 'You have exactly 1,927 sheep here.'

The shepherd answered, 'You are right. Pick out a sheep.'

The man took one of the animals and put it in the back of his vehicle. The shepherd looked at him and asked, 'If I guess your profession, will you pay me back in kind?'

'Sure.'

'You're a consultant.'

'Exactly! How on earth did you know that?' asked the man.

'Simple,' replied the shepherd. 'First you came without being invited. Secondly, you charged me for telling me something I already knew. Thirdly, you know nothing about my business, and I'd really like to have my dog back.'